Cordon Bleu

Soups and Starters

Cordon Bleu

Soups and Starters

Macdonald and Jane's
London

Published by
Macdonald and Jane's Publishers Ltd
Paulton House
8 Shepherdess Walk
London N1

Copyright B.P.C. Publishing Ltd., 1972

This impression 1977

Designed by Melvin Kyte
Printed by Waterlow (Dunstable) Ltd

These recipes have been adapted from the Cordon Bleu Cookery Course
published by Purnell in association with the London Cordon Bleu
Cookery School
Principal : Rosemary Hume ; Co-Principal : Muriel Downes

Quantities given are for 4 servings unless more are specified.
Spoon measures are level unless otherwise stated.

Contents

Introduction

There is a school of thought, perhaps centred around Vienna, that says no three or four course meal can start with anything except soup. Others of us prefer to ring the changes with a light, appetising dish of some other type. The Italians serve pasta as a first course — a dish often regarded in Britain as a substantial main course. In this book of soups and starters we have tried to cater for all tastes and give as wide a variety of dishes as possible.

Many cooks fight shy of making their own soups because they feel this will be expensive and time-consuming. In fact, it's quite the opposite. As well as an attractive starter for a party meal, soups are a good standby for everyday meals. They are economical to make because they can usually be varied to include whatever ingredients you have in the home.

And if you don't fancy soup, in this book there are over sixty other starters from which you can choose. Fish, egg and salad dishes, a selection of pâtés and some tasty suggestions for a mixed hors d'œuvre should help you vary the menu when you are entertaining.

In the appendix we have included a glossary of some of the special cooking terms used, and notes on the preparation of various items that recur at intervals through the book. Experienced cooks may not need to use this, but if there is a basic item or cooking term with which you are not familiar, you will find if further explained in the appendix. We should also particularly like you to look at the instructions for preparing shellfish because it is so important that they be thoroughly cleaned.

A good first course is the herald of a good meal. We wish you every success with your dinners, and hope you will have fun experimenting with some of our favourite Cordon Bleu starters.

Rosemary Hume
Muriel Downes

Hot soups

Warm and delicious, a tasty starter or a nourishing meal, easily made and easy to store for several days — what more could a cook want ? Yet soups are sadly neglected in the average English kitchen. There are so many good canned and packet varieties on the market that cooks tend to feel they need not compete ; whereas the very originality of a home-made soup will delight all comers.

For soup to be really useful, make it in large quantities. It will keep in the refrigerator for 3-4 days, as long as cream has not been added. A bowlful followed by bread and cheese makes a quick and nourishing lunch — and you will find the family disappointed if it comes up only once as a starter to a main meal.

A blender is invaluable if you wish to make velvety, well-flavoured soups. This is a gadget that really does make nothing of home soup-making. Occasionally though, you will need to sieve rather than blend a purée soup — to remove such things as tomato seeds — and for this a Mouli sieve with a fine disc is better. A Mouli can be used for all cream soups if you have no blender, though it will take a little longer.

First set the Mouli sieve over the bowl and pour the liquid through. Then tip in the solids to be sieved half at a time. Work the handle until it is all through before adding the second portion. It is most important that every bit goes through the sieve, otherwise the soup will lack flavour and will be too thin.

If sieving a thick soup such as bean or potato, first sieve the solids into a fresh bowl and then dilute gradually with the liquid to avoid lumps. If you haven't a Mouli, rub the soup through an ordinary wire sieve with a wooden spoon.

The basis of most good soups is stock. In an emergency a bouillon cube may be used, but it can never replace the real thing because it will lack the characteristic jellied quality. Bouillon cubes are salty and there is always a risk of over-seasoning. If you use bouillon cubes too often, your soups will have a monotonous flavour and the bouillon cube taste will give you away. (See opposite for stock recipes).

Many soups are bound with a liaison, either egg yolks and cream, slaked arrowroot or kneaded butter. Add these carefully to prevent the soup going lumpy or curdling.

Egg yolks and cream. This mixture may be used to thicken and enrich some cream soups. The yolk or yolks are worked well together with the cream. 2-3 tablespoons of soup are blended into the mixture, a little at a time, and when well blended the whole is returned to the main bulk of the soup and stirred in gradually. Reheat, stirring continually, but do not boil. This will cook the egg yolks slowly and so give a particularly creamy consistency.

Fécule, ie. arrowroot or potato flour, should be slaked (mixed) with water or milk and stirred into the nearly boiling liquid off the heat. Once added, reboil and draw aside.

Kneaded butter (beurre manié) is a liaison mixture of butter and flour in the proportions of almost twice as much butter to flour, worked together on a plate with a fork to make a paste.

Kneaded butter should be added to hot (but not boiling) liquids. Shake pan gently and when the butter has dissolved (indicating flour has been absorbed in liquid) reboil. If the liquid is still not thick enough, the process can be repeated.

Stocks
Mixed stock

If you want a really clear stock, the only way to make it is to use raw bones. If you are using cooked ones as well, it helps to add these after the stock has come to the boil, although it is better not to mix raw with cooked bones if the stock is to be kept for any length of time.

Any trimmings or leftovers in the way of meat can go into your regular stockpot : chicken carcasses and giblets (but not the liver) ; bacon rinds ; or a ham or bacon bone. This last is often given away and it makes excellent stock for a pea soup.

Add a plateful of cut-up root vegetables, a bouquet garni, 5-6 peppercorns, and pour in enough cold water to cover the ingredients by two-thirds. Salt very lightly, or not at all if there is a bacon bone in the pot. Bring slowly to the boil, skim, half-cover the pan and simmer $1\frac{1}{2}$-2 hours or longer, depending on the quantity of stock being made. The liquid should reduce by about a third. Strain off and, when the stock is cold, skim well to remove any fat. Throw away the ingredients unless a fair amount of raw bones have been used, in which case more water can be added and a second boiling made.

If the stock is to be kept several days, or if there is a fair proportion of chicken in it, bring to the boil every day. Remember that the stronger the stock, the better it will keep.

Watchpoint Long slow simmering is essential for any meat stock. It should never be allowed to boil hard as this will result in a thick muddy-looking jelly instead of a semi-clear one.

Brown bone stock

3 lb beef bones (or mixed
   beef / veal)
2 onions (quartered)
2 carrots (quartered)
1 stick of celery
large bouquet garni
6 peppercorns
3-4 quarts water
salt

*6-quart capacity saucepan, or small
   fish kettle*

Method
Wipe bones but do not wash
unless unavoidable. Put into a
very large pan. Set on gentle
heat and leave bones to fry
gently for 15-20 minutes.
Enough fat will come out from
the marrow so do not add any to
pan unless bones are very dry.

After 10 minutes add the
vegetables, having sliced the
celery into 3-4 pieces.

When bones and vegetables
are just coloured, add herbs,
peppercorns and the water,
which should come up two-
thirds above level of ingredients.
Bring slowly to the boil, skimming occasionally, then half
cover pan to allow reduction to
take place and simmer 4-5
hours, or until stock tastes
strong and good. For a strong
beef broth, add 1 lb shin of
beef to the pot halfway through
the cooking.

White bone stock
This stock is made in the same
way as brown bone stock, except
that bones and vegetables are
not browned before the water is
added, and veal bones are used.
Do not add the vegetables until
the bones have come to the boil
and the fat has been skimmed
off the liquid.

Vegetable stock

1 lb carrots
1 lb onions
$\frac{1}{2}$ head of celery
$\frac{1}{2}$ oz butter
3-4 peppercorns
1 teaspoon tomato purée
2 quarts water
salt

Method
Quarter vegetables, brown
lightly in the butter in a large
pan. Add peppercorns, tomato
purée, water and salt. Bring to
boil, cover pan and simmer 2
hours or until the stock has a
good flavour.

Chicken stock
This should ideally be made
from the giblets (neck, gizzard,
heart and feet, if available), but
never the liver which imparts a
bitter flavour. This is better
kept for making pâté, or sautéd
and used as a savoury. Dry fry
the giblets with an onion,
washed but not peeled, and cut
in half. To dry fry, use a thick
pan with a lid, with barely
enough fat to cover the bottom.
Allow the pan to get very hot
before putting in the giblets
and onion, cook on full heat
until lightly coloured. Remove
pan from heat before covering
with 2 pints of cold water. Add
a large pinch of salt, a few
peppercorns and a bouquet
garni (bayleaf, thyme, parsley)
and simmer gently for 1-2 hours.
Alternatively, make the stock
when you cook the chicken by
putting the giblets in the roasting
tin around the chicken with the
onion and herbs, and use the
measured quantity of water.

11

Garnishes for soups

Croûtons

2-3 rounds of stale bread, crusts removed (makes enough for 4 servings)
mixture of butter and oil (for frying)

Method
Cut the bread in small dice and fry in shallow fat deep enough to cover them (about $\frac{1}{2}$-$\frac{3}{4}$ inch deep); fat must be at frying heat when croûtons are added. Turn them to brown evenly (this will take only a few seconds). Remove croûtons with a draining spoon, drain on absorbent paper, shake off excess fat and sprinkle with salt before serving.

Frying can be done ahead of time and croûtons reheated for 1-2 minutes in a hot oven.

Serve separately with cream or purée soups.

Potato croûtons

These are especially good with spinach, tomato or celery soup.

Parboil 2 potatoes, drain and cut into dice while hot. Fry and serve as for bread croûtons.

Cheese croûtes

Any leftover cream sauce, cheese or onion, makes a good croûte. Toast bread on one side, spread the untoasted side with sauce and sprinkle well with grated cheese. Brown well under the grill. Cut in half and then into strips. Serve hot separately with soup.

SAVOURY BUTTERS

When these mixtures are made, pat into balls with butter 'hands' (wooden shaping boards), or spread $\frac{1}{4}$-$\frac{1}{2}$ inch thick on greaseproof paper and chill. Then cut into small round or square pats before using. The quantities given are enough for 4 people. Serve with bland soups such as potato or celery.

Maître d'hôtel butter

2 oz unsalted butter
1 dessertspoon chopped parsley
few drops of lemon juice
salt and pepper

Method
Soften the butter on a plate with a palette knife, then add parsley, lemon juice and seasoning to taste.

Serve chilled, in pats.

Cheese butter

Work grated cheese into a little butter, add plenty of pepper and a little salt and shape into pats. Serve chilled.

Cream of watercress soup

2 bunches of watercress
1 oz butter
1 medium-size onion (chopped)
1 rounded tablespoon plain flour
1½ pints milk
salt and pepper
5 tablespoons single cream
2 egg yolks or 1 teaspoon
   arrowroot (mixed to a paste with
   2-3 tablespoons top of milk, or
   single cream)
croûtons of fried bread

Method

Wash the watercress, remove any fine hairs but do not trim away the stalks, and shred finely. Melt butter in a saucepan, add watercress and onion, cover with greaseproof paper and lid and stew gently for 10 minutes. Draw aside and blend in flour. Bring milk to the boil, pour on to the watercress mixture and season. Simmer for 15 minutes, then pass through a Mouli sieve, or make into a purée in an electric blender. Return soup to the saucepan, thicken with liaison.

The ingredients for this delicious cream of watercress soup are simple and inexpensive

To make liaison of egg yolks and cream : first work yolks and cream together in a small basin, stir in 2 tablespoons hot soup and then return this to the saucepan in a thin, steady stream (stirring all the time) and re-heat very slowly until soup thickens. Adjust seasoning, serve croûtons separately.

Watchpoint When entertaining, there is always the problem of keeping the soup hot, and using an egg yolk liaison increases the danger of curdling. If your guests are likely to be late, thicken the soup with the arrowroot paste instead, turning out the heat under the soup. Have waiting a warm tureen and, when ready to serve, bring soup to the boil once more and tip the cream straight into the tureen. Then whisk the boiling soup into the cream and serve at once with croûtons.

Tomato and orange soup

2 lb tomatoes
1 onion (sliced)
1 carrot (sliced)
1 strip of lemon rind
1 bayleaf
6 peppercorns
salt
chicken bones, or
   1 chicken bouillon cube (for stock)
2 pints water (for stock)
$1\frac{1}{2}$ oz butter
3-4 tablespoons plain flour
rind and juice of $\frac{1}{2}$ orange
pepper
granulated sugar (to taste)
$\frac{1}{4}$ pint single cream

Use ripe tomatoes when they are at their best. At other times use a large can of Italian tomatoes to get the best flavour.

Method

First wipe the tomatoes and cut in half, squeezing to remove the seeds. Put tomatoes, onion and carrot into a pan with lemon rind, bayleaf, peppercorns and a good pinch of salt. Then make the stock : put chicken bones or bouillon cube into pan with 2 pints water and a pinch of salt. Bring to the boil and then reduce liquid by a quarter by simmering. Add stock to tomato mixture, put lid on and simmer until tomatoes are pulpy (about 30 minutes), then rub through a sieve and set aside.

Clean the pan, melt the butter in it, and stir in the flour. Pour on the tomato mixture, blend and bring to the boil. Shred the orange rind, blanch by cooking in boiling water for 1 minute, then drain, rinse well with cold water and set aside. Now add the orange juice to soup, then seasoning and sugar to taste. Stir in the cream at the last moment and finally add the orange rind. Serve at once.

Tomato and rice soup

1 lb ripe tomatoes
1 clove of garlic (bruised)
2 bayleaves
2 oz butter
2 onions (finely sliced)
1 dessertspoon plain flour
1½ pints vegetable stock, or water
1 lump of sugar
salt
black pepper (ground from mill)
1 rounded tablespoon long grain rice
2 slices of bread
½ oz cheese (grated)
½ teaspoon French mustard

Method

Take three-quarters of the tomatoes, scald, skin, quarter and flick out the seeds. Put into a pan with the bruised clove of garlic, bayleaves and ¾ oz butter. Cover and simmer slowly for about 10 minutes. Rub through a sieve to a purée.

Put the sliced onions in a stewpan with another ¾ oz butter, cover and cook slowly for 15 minutes. Remove from heat, add the flour, stock or water, and puréed tomatoes. Add sugar and season. Add the rice and simmer for 20-30 minutes.

Scald and skin the remaining tomatoes. Cut into quarters, discard the seeds, cut flesh into shreds and add to the soup.

Toast the bread on one side only. Mix remaining ½ oz butter, cheese and mustard together, then spread on the untoasted side of the bread. Brown under the grill. Cut into strips and serve hot with the soup.

Cream of tomato soup

1½ lb ripe tomatoes
1 onion
1 carrot
1 oz butter
1 rounded tablespoon plain flour
1½ pints light stock, or water
bouquet garni
salt, pepper and sugar (to taste)
cream, or evaporated milk
   (optional)
chives (optional)

For liaison (optional)
1 dessertspoon arrowroot
2-3 tablespoons cold water

Method

Slice onion and carrot. Wipe tomatoes, cut in half and squeeze to remove seeds. Strain the seeds through a strainer and retain juice.

Melt butter in a pan, put in onion and carrot, cover and cook gently for about 5 minutes. Draw off the heat, stir in the flour, add tomatoes, juice from seeds and stock or water. Bring to the boil, add bouquet garni and season to taste. Simmer for 30 minutes.

Take out the bouquet garni and rub soup through a strainer or Mouli sieve. Rinse out pan, return soup to it and reheat.

If soup is too thin, thicken with the arrowroot slaked with cold water. Stir this in quickly while soup is at boiling point.

A tablespoon of cream or evaporated milk may be added to each dish of soup and a few snipped chives sprinkled on top.

Soup Georgette

5-6 ripe tomatoes
1 small head of celery (finely sliced)
2 leeks (finely sliced)
$\frac{1}{2}$ lb carrots (finely sliced)
1 oz butter
1 oz plain flour
2 pints water
pinch of granulated sugar
$\frac{1}{2}$ bayleaf
pinch of ground nutmeg
salt and pepper
5 tablespoons top of milk
parsley (chopped)

For liaison (optional)
1 teaspoon arrowroot
1 tablespoon water

Method

Scald, skin and remove seeds from tomatoes, strain seeds and reserve juice and flesh. Prepare the vegetables and sweat them in the butter. Stir in flour and then add tomato flesh, juice from the seeds, water, sugar, $\frac{1}{2}$ bayleaf, nutmeg and seasoning. Stir mixture until boiling and then simmer for 30 minutes.

Sieve the mixture and return to the pan to reheat. If necessary, thicken slightly with arrowroot (slaked with a little water). Adjust seasoning, simmer for a few seconds, then stir in the top of milk.

Sprinkle well with chopped parsley before serving.

Soup Georgette has a tomato base, enriched with celery, leeks and carrots

16

Consommé madrilène

3 pints chicken stock
$\frac{3}{4}$ lb lean shin of beef (finely
   shredded)
1 lb ripe tomatoes (skinned,
   seeds removed and sliced)
2 $\frac{1}{2}$ fl oz sherry, or Madeira
whites and shells (wiped and
   crushed) of 2 eggs
1 rounded dessertspoon tomato
   purée (optional)
extra sherry (optional)
1 extra tomato (skinned, seeds
   removed, and cut in fine shreds)
   — to garnish

Consommé madrilène, a clear soup,
is made on a base of chicken stock.
It is garnished with strips of tomato

Method

Put the stock into a thick enamel, or tinlined, pan. Add the beef, tomatoes and the sherry (or Madeira). Using a metal whisk (any other type of whisk and pan would make the consommé cloudy), whip egg whites to a light froth and add to liquid with the crushed shells ; whisk backwards, over moderate heat, until the liquid is at boiling point. Then stop whisking and allow the soup to come up to the top of the pan. Draw pan aside, allow liquid to subside, then replace on heat and boil up carefully once more, taking care not to break the 'filter' (froth of egg whites) which will form on top. Draw pan aside and leave for 40 minutes on very low heat to extract all the flavour from the meat.

Place a scalded cloth over a bowl and pour the soup through, at first keeping the 'filter' back with a spoon and then, at the end, sliding it out on to the cloth. Pour the soup again through the cloth and the 'filter'. Consommé should now be clear ; if not, pour through the cloth again. If wished, add tomato purée to give a little colour and additional flavour. The best way to do this is to put the purée in a bowl and pour on the soup. Add extra sherry, if wished. Reheat consommé for serving, but do not boil, and add the prepared garnish.

Potage madrilène

2 pints chicken stock (cold)
1 medium-size onion (finely chopped)
1 oz butter
1 large can (1 lb 12 oz) Italian plum tomatoes
bouquet garni (containing a strip of lemon rind)
salt (to taste)
6 black peppercorns (to taste)
5 fl oz sherry
1 tablespoon arrowroot (slaked with 2 tablespoons water)
squeeze of lemon juice
1 small carton (2 $\frac{1}{2}$ fl oz) single cream
1 tablespoon fresh snipped chives

It is important to have the stock as free from fat as possible, and grease can only be removed completely if the stock is at refrigerator temperature.

A spoonful of cream in each serving is decorative as well as delicious

Method

Skim the stock thoroughly. Cook the onion slowly in butter in a pan until soft but not coloured, add stock, tomatoes, bouquet garni, salt and peppercorns. Stir until boiling, crushing tomatoes with wooden spoon, cover and simmer for 40 minutes. Pass through a Mouli sieve or rub through a nylon strainer.

Watchpoint These methods are better than using an electric blender, as the latter breaks down the seeds. Both flavour and appearance are improved if the seeds are removed by straining.

Return the soup to the rinsed-out pan, boil the sherry until reduced to half and add to soup. Thicken very slightly with the arrowroot. Reboil, add lemon juice and adjust the seasoning.

A spoonful of cream should be floated on top of each soup cup or plate as it is served; sprinkle with fresh snipped chives.

Potage bonne femme

6 leeks
4 small potatoes
$2\frac{1}{2}$ oz butter
salt
pepper (ground from mill)
$\frac{3}{4}$ pint milk
$\frac{3}{4}$ pint water
2 egg yolks
$\frac{1}{4}$ pint single cream
1 teaspoon chopped parsley
croûtons of fried bread

Method

Wash and trim leeks very carefully as they can be gritty. Make a deep cross-cut through the leaves and wash under a fast-running tap. Slice the white parts only of 5 leeks, keeping the other aside for garnish. Peel and slice potatoes.

Melt the butter in a large pan, add the vegetables and seasoning and stir over a gentle heat until almost soft. When vegetables are well impregnated with the butter and have started to cook, cover them with a buttered paper and lid (this is known as sweating) ; there is no need to stir them all the time. Cook for at least 10 minutes.

Pour on the milk and water and stir until boiling. Draw pan half off heat and half cover the pan with a lid ; leave to simmer for 15 minutes.

Pass soup through a Mouli sieve or mix to a purée in an electric blender.

Cut the reserved leek into fine shreds with a knife, put into cold water and boil for 2 minutes. Drain and dry.

Return soup to clean pan and reheat. Work the egg yolks with cream in a bowl and add about 3-4 tablespoons of hot soup to this liaison. Pour this back into pan in a thin, steady stream and stir over a gentle heat until the soup thickens.

Watchpoint Do not let soup boil or the eggs will curdle. If this should happen, whisking will help the appearance.

Garnish soup with a little shredded leek and chopped parsley ; serve the croûtons separately.

Mulligatawny

1 lb lean mutton, or lamb (a piece
of double scrag is suitable)
2 onions
1 carrot
1 small cooking apple
1 large tablespoon dripping, or
butter
1 dessertspoon curry powder
1 rounded teaspoon curry paste
1 rounded tablespoon plain flour
2½ pints cold water
¼ pint milk
few drops of lemon juice

For liaison (optional)
little arrowroot
1-2 tablespoons water

This soup can be made from any kind of meat or trimmings of meat.

A good stock can be used instead of water in mulligatawny ; in this case the meat will not be needed. For a richer soup, add a little cream to the milk.

A curry paste adds to the flavour ; it is more spicy and blander than a curry powder and the two mix well together. This mixture, though not essential, is often used in curries.

Method

Soak meat for 1 hour in salted water. Slice vegetables and peel, core and slice apple. Wipe and dry meat. Melt the fat in a pan and brown the meat lightly in it. Remove meat, add vegetables and apple ; cook for 3-4 minutes. Add curry powder, fry for 2-3 seconds, then add paste.

Watchpoint The curry powder must be fried for 2-3 seconds to ensure that it is cooked.

After 2 minutes stir in the flour and pour on the water. Bring to the boil and add the meat. Cover and cook gently for 1-1½ hours. Then take out the meat and sieve or blend liquid and vegetables. If using an electric blender, add some of the meat, reserving a little for a garnish, if liked.

Rinse out pan, pour in blended soup, add the milk and bring to the boil. Add lemon juice. If you have sieved the soup, it may be necessary to thicken it with a little arrowroot slaked in cold water.

Game soup 1

1-2 pigeons and / or wings (forelegs)
   and trimmings of 1 hare
$2\frac{1}{2}$ oz butter
1 onion (sliced)
1 carrot (sliced)
2 sticks of celery (sliced)
bouquet garni
$2\frac{1}{2}$ pints brown stock, or water
salt and pepper
2-3 flat, dark mushrooms
   (sliced)
$1\frac{1}{4}$ oz plain flour
1 wineglass red wine, or sherry

A good soup can be made out of a comparatively small quantity of game. If brown stock is not available, add 6-8 oz of lean shin of beef to strengthen the flavour.

Method

Wipe the game and brown it in 1 oz butter in a pan. Remove from pan and split each pigeon in two. If using beef, brown this also and cut into pieces. Remove from pan.

Prepare the onion, carrot and celery and cook in the butter until brown ; add game and meat, bouquet garni and stock or water. Season, cover pan and simmer for $1-1\frac{1}{2}$ hours.

Strain the soup. Cut some game into shreds and set aside for garnish. Measure liquid — there should be about 2 pints. Melt $\frac{3}{4}$ oz butter in the pan, put in the prepared mushrooms and cook briskly for 2-3 minutes, then add rest of butter and stir in the flour. Add wine, or sherry, and soup and stir until boiling.

Adjust seasoning and simmer for 5 minutes. Add shredded game and serve.

Game soup 2

carcass of 1 pheasant, or 2 grouse
   (cooked)
1 large onion (stuck with a clove)
1 clove of garlic (unpeeled)
4 carrots (peeled and quartered)
1 turnip (peeled and quartered)
bouquet garni (containing a stick
   of celery)
9 peppercorns
pinch of salt
6 pints brown stock
4-6 oz cold cooked game meat
2-3 oz fresh white breadcrumbs
pinch of ground mace
1 glass golden sherry
$\frac{1}{4}$ pint double cream
3 egg yolks
croûtons of fried bread

This quantity serves 12 people.

Method

Cut the carcass into small pieces with kitchen or game scissors and put into a large pan with the vegetables, bouquet garni, peppercorns, salt and the brown stock. Cover pan and simmer gently for 2-3 hours until stock is well flavoured and reduced to about half its quantity ; strain.

Chop the game meat quite finely and mix with the breadcrumbs, moistened with about $\frac{1}{2}$ pint stock, and pound or work in the liquidiser to a smooth paste. Dilute this mixture with the rest of the stock, return it to the rinsed-out pan, season, add the mace and bring to the boil. Then add the sherry.

Beat the cream into the egg yolks with a wooden spoon, add 2-3 tablespoons of the hot soup to this liaison, mix well and then return to the soup very slowly, stirring all the time. Reheat soup carefully without boiling and serve croûtons separately.

Chowder

6 oz piece of streaky bacon
(unsmoked)
1 oz butter
2 sticks of celery (finely sliced)
1 onion (finely sliced)
2 medium-size potatoes (diced)
1 pint water
1 bayleaf
salt and pepper
1 rounded tablespoon plain flour
1 pint milk
1 packet frozen sweetcorn
kernels, or 1 small can sweetcorn
1 rounded dessertspoon chopped
parsley

Method
Discard rind and rust and cut
bacon into small dice. Blanch
and drain. Melt butter in a pan,
add bacon and fry gently until
it begins to change colour.
Then add the celery and onion.
Cook for 1 minute, then add the
potatoes, water and bayleaf.
Season lightly and cook gently
until the potatoes are tender
(about 20 minutes). Remove the
pan from the heat.

Mix the flour with a little of
the milk and stir into the soup.
Add rest of milk and the sweetcorn. Bring to the boil and
simmer for 10-15 minutes.

Serve sprinkled with a little
chopped parsley.

This chowder is a thick, filling broth made mainly from bacon and potatoes

Scallop chowder

4 large scallops
4 oz long grain rice
about 1 oz butter
1 medium-size onion (finely
    chopped)
4 oz streaky bacon rashers (rind
    and rust removed — cut into
    strips)
1 small head of celery (finely
    sliced)
1 small can (8 oz) tomatoes
about 1½ pints boiling water
large pinch of saffron (infused in
    2 tablespoons hot water for
    about 30 minutes)
salt
pepper (ground from mill)
1 tablespoon chopped parsley

Method
Soak the rice in a little cold water for about 30 minutes and then drain. Melt the butter in a large saucepan, put in the onion and bacon and fry gently for a few minutes, then add the rice and continue to fry gently for 1-2 minutes more. Add the celery, tomatoes, boiling water and saffron. Season, partially cover the pan and simmer until the rice is very tender, about 15-20 minutes.

Slice the scallops crosswise (see page 139) and add them to the soup. Taste for seasoning and continue to simmer for a further 15-20 minutes. Just before serving stir in the parsley.
Note : if wished, a glass of white wine may be added in place of an equal quantity of the boiling water. The chowder should be fairly thick but not too much so ; more liquid should be added if too much reduction takes place.

The main ingredients from which scallop chowder will be made

Mussel chowder

1 can mussels (14 oz)
4 oz green streaky bacon
1 large onion (chopped)
1 stick of celery (chopped)
1 green pepper (blanched and
  chopped)
2 medium-size potatoes (diced)
1 small bayleaf
$\frac{3}{4}$ pint water
salt and pepper
$1\frac{1}{4}$ oz plain flour
1 pint milk
1 dessertspoon chopped parsley

Chowder, an American speciality, is a soup stew made from shellfish (or white fish) with vegetables and unsmoked bacon or salt pork, according to the recipe. Another version, using bacon and potatoes (without fish) is given on page 22.

It was introduced to the United States by early French settlers, and the word originates either from 'chaudrée de Fouras', a fish soup from the Fouras region of France, or from 'chaudière' (kettle).

Method

Remove the rind and cut bacon into dice ; sizzle gently in a dry pan until turning colour, then add the onion and celery and cook until golden-brown. Add the green pepper, potatoes, bayleaf and water and bring to the boil. Season, and simmer until potatoes are tender, then draw pan aside.

Blend the flour with $\frac{1}{2}$ cup of the milk and add to the chowder ; stir until boiling. Heat the rest of the milk and add to the chowder with the drained mussels ; simmer for 4-5 minutes before turning into a soup tureen. Scatter parsley over top.

As shellfish are rather expensive in Britain, it is a good idea to use canned mussels for this chowder

Mussel chowder is richly flavoured with bacon, onion, celery and pepper

Mussel soup

1 quart mussels
1 lb sole bones
1 onion (sliced and blanched)
6 white peppercorns
$1\frac{1}{2}$ oz butter
bouquet garni
juice of $\frac{1}{2}$ lemon
salt
2 wineglasses white wine
1 clove of garlic
$1\frac{1}{4}$ pints stock, or water
1 rounded tablespoon plain flour
2 egg yolks
$2\frac{1}{2}$ fl oz double cream
1 dessertspoon chopped parsley

Method
Put the well-washed fish bones in a saucepan with onion, peppercorns, $\frac{1}{2}$ oz of butter, bouquet garni and lemon juice. Cover the pan and cook over very gentle heat for 10 minutes. Add salt, 1 glass of wine, garlic and stock or water and simmer for 20 minutes.

Melt 1 oz butter in a pan, stir in the flour and cook gently until straw-coloured, then strain fish stock on to this and bring to the boil. Simmer for 15 minutes.

Meanwhile, wash and scrub the mussels (see page 137), put into a pan with the rest of the wine. Bring to the boil, then strain the liquor into the soup.

Shell the mussels and discard the beards, add the mussels to the soup and simmer for 5 minutes. Mix egg yolks with cream, stir in 3-4 tablespoons of hot soup, then add this liaison to the soup. Reheat without boiling, add parsley and serve.

The cleaned mussels ready for cooking in wine to make mussel soup

Oyster soup

12 oysters, or 1 can of oysters
2 oz butter
2 shallots (finely chopped)
$\frac{1}{2}$ teaspoon paprika pepper
pinch of ground mace
1 tablespoon cornflour
1 can (about 12 oz) evaporated
  milk
$\frac{3}{4}$ pint milk
salt and pepper

Method
Melt the butter and add the shallots, cover and cook slowly until golden. Add the paprika and mace, cook for 1 minute then blend in the cornflour, evaporated milk and milk. Season and stir until boiling, then simmer for 3-4 minutes. Remove the oysters from their shells and add them, with any liquid (or canned ones with their juice), to the pan. Reheat carefully without boiling.

Oysters
Nowadays in Great Britain oysters are so expensive that fresh ones are considered a delicacy only to be eaten raw. This has not always been the case : in 1712 the best oysters sold for 3s. a barrel and the poor bought them from barrows in the streets. After about 1850 exploitation of the oyster beds and disease combined to raise the price of European oysters.

Lobster bisque

1 medium-size live lobster
3 oz butter
2 tablespoons oil
1 small onion (finely chopped)
1 wineglass sherry
2 pints fish stock

For velouté
$1\frac{1}{2}$ oz butter
$1\frac{1}{2}$ oz plain flour
salt and pepper
$\frac{1}{4}$ pint double cream

A can of lobster claw meat may be used, but to get the very best flavour use a live lobster.

Method
If you have a live lobster, kill and split it (see page 137) ; reserve the coral.

Make lobster butter by working the coral with $1\frac{1}{2}$ oz of the butter. Set this mixture aside.

Heat the oil and $1\frac{1}{2}$· oz butter in a large sauté pan. Put lobster in the pan, cover and cook for 5 minutes, then add onion and sherry. Cover and simmer for 10-15 minutes. Take up, remove meat from body and claws. **Note :** some of the tail meat may be reserved for garnish, in which case cut it in slices and add to soup just before serving.

Pound the meat or work it in an electric blender with a little of the stock.

To make velouté : melt the butter, stir in flour, pour on stock and any juices from lobster pan. Bring to the boil, season and simmer for 5-6 minutes ; draw aside. Add the pounded lobster and lobster butter (or $1\frac{1}{2}$ oz plain butter) in small pieces and reheat, adding the cream, but do not allow to boil. Serve at once.

Bouillabaisse

6-7 lb fish :
   Dublin Bay prawns, or small
      langoustes
   rock salmon (sometimes called
      'woof' in northern ports)
   conger eel
   turbot
   bass
   gurnet
   red and grey mullet
   whiting
$1\frac{1}{2}$ wineglasses olive oil
2 medium-size onions (chopped)
3 leeks (white part only, sliced)
4-5 large ripe tomatoes (skinned,
   chopped and seeds removed), or
   1 wineglass fresh tomato pulp
3-4 cloves of garlic (chopped)
bouquet garni (including 2-3
   sticks of fennel and a thinly
   pared strip of orange rind)
salt and pepper
pinch of saffron
2-3 quarts boiling water
1 long French loaf (to give about
   20 slices)
2-3 rounded tablespoons freshly
   chopped parsley

This rich fish soup is a speciality of the Mediterranean coast and the best is found in those parts where a variety of fresh fish can be obtained.

Unfortunately it is not possible to make a true bouillabaisse away from this region as some of the fish, especially the rascasse, which is considered essential, are only caught in the Mediterranean.

However, it is possible to make a good imitation if a variety of fish is available. Apart from the freshness of the fish, the secret of a good bouillabaisse is rapid cooking. In this way the quantity of oil used is incorporated in the liquid and so does not rise to the top. A mixture of firm- and tender-fleshed fish is used, such as the conger eel, Dublin Bay prawns, langouste, whiting, red and grey mullet, gurnet etc. Owing to the amount of fish necessary for the soup, it is generally enough for 8-10 people and is a good dish for an informal party. It is served in two dishes, one containing the pieces of fish and the other a terrine with slices of French bread, which thicken the soup, well impregnated with the broth.

Bouillabaisse is served piping hot and is a meal in itself. This recipe is from Marseille, but the varieties of fish have been altered to those available in this country.

For 8-10 people, about 6-7 lb fish is necessary, including shellfish. The actual amount of each kind may be taken according to availability.

Method

Clean the fish well and slice the firm-fleshed fish (ie. all except the prawns or langoustes).

Choose a large, roomy stew pan ; set it on full heat and pour in the oil. Add the chopped onion and sliced leeks, stir and cook for 1 minute only ; do not allow to brown. Add the tomatoes, garlic, bouquet garni, and firm-fleshed fish. Season, add the saffron, then pour on the boiling water, enough to cover the fish. Bring to the boil as quickly as possible, with the lid off the pan. Boil hard for 10 minutes ; do not stir, but shake the pan gently from time to time to make sure the fish is not sticking to the bottom. Now put in the tender-fleshed fish and cook for a further 5 minutes only. Total cooking time must not exceed 15 minutes, but see that the liquid, by boiling strongly, covers the pieces of fish on the top. Give the pan a sideways shake occasionally to prevent the fish from sticking.

Meanwhile slice the bread into 18-20 pieces and put them in the bottom of a terrine or deep dish. At the end of the cooking time, draw the pan aside and strain about three-quarters of the fish broth over the bread ; reserve rest of the liquid. Cover and keep hot.

Transfer the strained fish as quickly as possible to the second dish, arranging pieces so that the different kinds are separated. Then baste any liquid in the terrine over the pieces of bread ; if it has all been absorbed, add the rest of the broth. The soup should, however, be thick with bread.

Sprinkle both dishes with the chopped parsley and serve.

Bouillabaisse is a Mediterranean speciality, but you can imitate it if there is a good variety of English fish available

Cream of fish soup

¾ lb fresh haddock fillet, or whiting
1½ oz butter
1½ oz plain flour
¼ pint single cream

For stock
1 lb sole bones, or 1 turbot's head
1 large onion (peeled and sliced)
½ oz butter
1 carrot (sliced)
1 stick of celery (sliced)
2 pints water
bouquet garni
½ teaspoon salt
6 peppercorns
1 wineglass dry white wine
slice of lemon

For garnish
2 sprigs of parsley, or chervil
croûtons of fried bread

Method

First prepare the stock. Wash the sole bones or turbot's head well, drain and set aside. Cover the onion with cold water, bring to the boil, drain and refresh. Melt ½ oz butter in a large saucepan, put in the onion with the fish bones or head on top, cover and cook slowly for 5 minutes. Add the sliced vegetables to the pan, pour over the water, add bouquet garni, seasoning, wine and lemon and simmer very gently for 20 minutes. Strain, measure 1¾ pints of the fish stock and set it aside.

Wash and dry the haddock or whiting, remove skin and then poach gently in the remaining fish stock. This can be done in a saucepan on top of the stove or in the oven at 350°F or Mark 4 for about 10 minutes. Remove the bones and pound the fish, or work in an electric blender, to a fine purée.

Melt the 1½ oz butter, stir in

the flour and cook very gently to a pale straw colour. Blend in the reserved stock and stir until boiling, then simmer for 5-10 minutes. Whisk in cream and fish purée ; taste for seasoning.

Break the parsley or chervil into sprigs and blanch for 1 minute in boiling water, then add to the soup.

Serve the croûtons separately.

Cream of fish soup is garnished with parsley, and served with croûtons

Cream of onion soup (Le tourin)

2 medium-size onions (thinly sliced)
good $1\frac{1}{2}$ oz butter
1 rounded tablespoon plain flour
$1\frac{3}{4}$ pints creamy milk
salt and pepper
2 eggs
2-3 tablespoons cream
4 thin slices of bread (for serving)

This is a regional dish from the Ile de France.

Method

Melt the butter, add the onion, cover the pan and cook slowly until soft. Do not allow the onion to colour. Draw the pan aside, stir in the flour and bring the milk to boil in a separate pan. Add the milk by degrees, blending it in well, then season.

Return pan to the heat and stir until boiling. Simmer for 8-12 minutes, then draw pan aside. Break the eggs into a large bowl and beat to a froth with the cream ; pour the hot soup on to them, whisking all the time. Adjust seasoning, set aside and keep warm.

Have ready the bread stamped out into rounds about 1 inch in diameter and bake these (in a moderate oven, set at 350°F or Mark 4) to a pale golden-brown. To serve, pour the soup into a tureen or individual bowls and place the rounds of bread on top.

French onion soup (Soupe à l'oignon)

5 onions
2 oz butter
$2\frac{1}{2}$ pints good bouillon
salt and pepper
1-2 glasses Champagne (optional)
3 oz each of Gruyère and Parmesan cheese (grated)
1 slice of French bread per person
1 egg per person (for serving)

This is perhaps the most famous of all French soups. The simple version is given on page 34 and is one of the best everyday soups. However, when made as 'haute cuisine' it is quite a different matter. The soup is made in much the same way, but a good bouillon is used in place of water. Moreover, a glass or two of Champagne, preferably flat, is added.

This quantity serves 6-8 people.

Method

Have ready small earthenware soup pots with lids (marmites). Slice or chop the onions finely and colour them to a golden-brown in butter in a frying pan. Bring the bouillon to the boil and add the onions ; season, simmer for 5 minutes, then add the Champagne, if using it.

Mix the cheeses together and sprinkle a little on the slices of bread ; put a slice into each marmite, then pour on the boiling soup. Put on the lids and serve. Alongside each place have a small dish of the remaining cheese and a fresh egg. Each guest breaks the raw egg into the soup, adds the cheese and beats it up with a fork. The soup must be really boiling so that the egg cooks a little and thickens the broth slightly.

Simple French onion soup

8 oz onions
1½ oz butter
1 tablespoon plain flour
2 pints stock, or water
salt and pepper
1 bayleaf
1-2 rolls (sliced), or 2 slices of
    stale bread (cut into four)
grated Cheddar, or Gruyère

Method

Chop onions. Heat a pan, drop in the butter and when foaming put in the onions. Lower heat and cook onions slowly for 15-20 minutes until golden-brown, stirring occasionally with a metal spoon. Stir in the flour and cook for a further 2-3 minutes. Heat stock or water to boiling point.

Watchpoint Take care when browning the onions; any scorching or burning spoils the flavour. This soup is improved by using a good stock but it holds its own even with water.

Draw pan aside, pour on boiling liquid, add seasoning and bayleaf. Simmer, uncovered, for 30 minutes.

Have a casserole ready with the sliced rolls laid on the bottom (or the bread slices cut into four). Pour in the boiling soup, first taking out bayleaf.

Scatter grated cheese thickly over the top and cook in the oven at 400°F or Mark 6 for 10 minutes or until brown. Serve in the casserole, or in individual pots.

This is a simpler version of the French onion soup

Potage parabère

4-5 medium-size onions (thinly
   sliced)
1½ oz butter
1¾ pints veal, or chicken, stock
salt and pepper
kneaded butter (see method)
1 dessertspoon chopped parsley
1 egg yolk
2½ fl oz single cream, or top of milk

For garnish
1 medium-size carrot
½ stick of celery
green part of leek

Method
Blanch the onions, drain
thoroughly and return to the
pan with the butter. Cover
tightly and cook slowly until soft ;
do not allow to colour. Draw
pan aside, pour off butter and
reserve it. Pour on the stock,
season, bring to the boil and
simmer until onion is very tender
(about 12-15 minutes).

Meanwhile make the garnish.
Cut the vegetables into thin
strips and cook until tender
(6-7 minutes) in a little boiling
salted water.

When ready, rub onion mixture
through a fine sieve or work in
a blender. Return onion purée
to the rinsed-out pan and thicken
a little with kneaded butter,
made with the reserved melted
butter and half as much flour.
The consistency of the soup
should be that of single cream.

Work the egg yolk with the
cream (or milk). Mix with 2
tablespoons of the hot soup,
add this liaison to the pan and
thicken slowly over the heat,
without allowing the soup to
boil. Draw aside and add the
parsley. Drain garnish and add
to the soup. Serve hot.

Potage parabère is garnished with julienne strips of vegetables

Garbure paysanne

1 medium-size turnip
2 medium-size carrots
$\frac{1}{2}$ small cabbage
2 medium-size onions
2 leeks (white part only)
1 small head of celery
2 medium-size potatoes
2-3 oz butter
1 cup cooked haricot beans
3-4 pints water, or stock
1 French roll, or small rounds of
bread (for croûtes)
1-2 oz Gruyère cheese
salt and pepper

Garbure, one of the classic soups of France, is a rustic or peasant vegetable soup, thick and substantial, so much so that it is frequently eaten as a main dish. A garbure is characterised by the croûtes of bread which are browned in butter and put on top of the soup before serving, or are served separately. The ingredients of garbure vary, as does the finishing of the croûtes, and this depends on where the garbure is made. For example, in the southern provinces, the croûtes are not always browned but are layered into the garbure.

This recipe is perhaps the most classic.

This quantity serves 6-8 people.

Method

Finely slice the raw vegetables. Choose a large stew pan, melt 1 oz butter in this and put in all the vegetables except the beans. Cover the pan and cook slowly for 15-20 minutes ; the vegetables must not brown. Add the beans and a good 2 pints of the water (or stock) ; this should well cover the vegetables — add more if necessary. Cover pan and simmer until vegetables are really tender.

Cut the French roll into slices and fry the bread in 1 oz of the butter until golden-brown ; set aside.

Take out 3 tablespoons of the vegetables with a draining spoon and pass them through a sieve or blender, then put in a pan with the remaining butter and cook until the consistency of mashed potato. Spread this purée over the croûtes, doming it up, and grate over the cheese. Set croûtes on a baking sheet and put to brown in a moderately hot oven.

Meanwhile put the rest of the soup through a sieve or blender ; add the remaining water (or stock) and continue to simmer until it becomes a smooth purée. Season well and, if wished, add a further ounce of butter in small pieces. Serve the soup very hot with the croûtes floating on top or served separately on a plate.

Crème St. Germain

12 spring onions (chopped)
the heart of 1 cabbage lettuce
(shredded)
1¾ pints well flavoured veal,
or chicken, stock
1 pint shelled peas (preferably
old and rather floury)
salt and pepper
1 oz butter
1 oz plain flour
1-2 egg yolks
2½ fl oz double cream

For garnish
½ pint young peas (shelled)
1 dessertspoon chopped mint

This green pea soup may also
be served iced. If you plan to do
this, you may omit the egg yolks
and increase the quantity of
cream to ¼ pint, lightly whip-
ping it before adding it to the
soup.

Method
Put onions and lettuce into a
pan with the stock and peas.
Season and bring to the boil.
Simmer until tender (about 20
minutes). Then rub the soup
through a Mouli sieve or work
in an electric blender. Melt the
butter in the rinsed-out pan,
add the flour and blend in the
liquid. Bring to the boil, cover
and simmer for 5—6 minutes.

Cook the young peas in water
until just tender, drain. Blend
the egg yolks and cream together, mix with 2-3 tablespoons
of the hot soup, then add this
liaison to the soup and reheat
without boiling. Add the peas
and sprinkle with the mint just
before serving.

Green pea soup

½ lb split green peas (soaked
overnight in water)
1½ oz butter
1 medium-size onion (thinly
sliced)
1 medium-size carrot (thinly
sliced)
1 clove of garlic (crushed with a
little salt)
2½-3 pints stock (it can be partly ham
stock, but not all, as this would
be far too salty)
salt and pepper
1 teaspoon granulated sugar
large pinch of dried mint, or
2-3 sprigs of fresh mint
2½ fl oz single cream (optional)

This quantity serves 4-6 people.

Method
Rinse the soaked peas, add
cold water to cover and bring
slowly to the boil. Salt lightly,
cover the pan and simmer for
about 1 hour ; set aside. Melt
1 oz of butter in a large pan,
add the onion and carrot and
the crushed garlic. Cover pan,
cook for 5 minutes, then add
the peas and their liquor and
a good half of the stock. Add
salt, pepper and sugar, then
simmer until all vegetables are
tender.

If during this time the soup
gets too thick, add more stock,
then rub through a fine sieve or
put through a blender. Return
to the rinsed-out pan, add the
mint and bring to the boil,
whisking well. Again adjust the
consistency, if necessary, by
adding a little more of the stock.
Simmer for 3-5 minutes, then
beat in the remaining butter and,
if using cream, streak it in to
give a marbled effect.

Minestra

1 carrot
1 onion
2 sticks of celery
2 tablespoons oil
about 2¼ pints water
½ bayleaf
1 small leek
6 French beans, or brussels sprouts
salt and pepper
2 small potatoes
1 clove of garlic
2 tomatoes
1 rounded dessertspoon chopped parsley
2-3 oz noodles (optional)
Parmesan cheese (grated)

Method

Cut the carrot, onion and celery into medium-thick julienne strips. Heat the oil in a stewpan, put in the vegetable strips and fry until just turning colour ; shake and stir occasionally.

Pour on water, add bayleaf. Cut leek, beans (or brussels sprouts) into shreds and add to the pan. Season lightly and simmer for 30-40 minutes.

Add potatoes, cut in strips, and simmer for a further 20 minutes. Crush garlic with a little salt. Scald tomatoes and skin, cut in quarters, flick out the seeds and cut flesh into strips or chop roughly. Add to the soup with the garlic and parsley, and noodles (if using). Simmer for a further 10 minutes, adjust seasoning and serve sprinkled with grated cheese.

More water should be added if necessary during the early stages of cooking if the soup seems over-thick.

Watchpoint To cut an onion into strips, cut in half down from crown to root. Lay onion, cut side downwards, on the board, slice fairly thinly, lengthways. The root, which holds the slices in place, can be trimmed off.

Minestra is a typical Italian soup. It is made from a variety of vegetables — cabbage, carrots, cauliflower, tomatoes, onions — in fact, any you have to hand in your kitchen or vegetable garden. Also, you can add a little pasta, such as spaghetti, macaroni, or small noodles

Minestrone

2 large tablespoons white
    haricot beans (soaked overnight
    in water)
2-3 pints stock
2 medium-size carrots
2-3 sticks of celery
1 large onion
2-3 tablespoons oil
2 leeks
2 rashers of fat bacon
1-2 cloves of garlic
$\frac{1}{4}$ small cabbage
1 small can tomatoes, or
    1 rounded dessertspoon
    tomato purée
bouquet garni
salt and pepper
Parmesan cheese (grated)

Method

Drain the beans, put in a pan
with about 1 pint of stock, bring
slowly to the boil and simmer
for at least 30 minutes. Meanwhile dice the carrots and slice
the celery and onion. Heat oil
in a stewpan, put in the carrot,
celery and onion and fry gently
for about 5 minutes.

Slice the leeks and cut bacon
into small pieces. Crush garlic
with a little salt and shred
cabbage.

Pour rest of the stock into
the pan and bring to the boil ;
add sliced leeks, bacon, tomatoes, or purée, garlic and the
bouquet garni. Season and
add the beans with their stock.
Simmer gently for 30 minutes,
then add the shredded cabbage.
Cook gently until the vegetables
are thoroughly cooked and
soup is of a good flavour.

A bowl of grated Parmesan
should be served separately.

Cream of beetroot soup

1 large beetroot (about $\frac{3}{4}$ lb) —
    cooked, skinned and grated
1 medium-size onion (finely
    chopped)
1 oz butter
$\frac{3}{4}$ oz plain flour
$1\frac{1}{4}$ pints well-flavoured chicken
    stock
salt and pepper
1 teaspoon red wine vinegar
$\frac{1}{2}$ teaspoon mustard (ready-made)
1 dessertspoon cornflour
3 tablespoons cream, or soured
    cream
1 tablespoon snipped chives
croûtons of fried bread

Method

Cook the onion in the butter until
it is soft ; add the flour, cook
it a few minutes until it is
marbled in appearance, then tip
on the stock. Bring this to the
boil, add the grated beetroot,
season well and add the wine
vinegar ; simmer gently for
about 20 minutes. Rub soup
through a sieve or purée in a
blender, and rinse out the pan.

Return soup to the rinsed-out
pan and season well with
mustard, salt and pepper as
necessary. Mix the cornflour
with the cream, add to the soup
and stir until it is boiling. Cook
soup for 3 minutes, then taste
for seasoning. Add the snipped
chives and serve with croûtons
of fried bread.

Cream of beetroot soup garnished
with snipped chives and croûtons

Vegetable bortsch

beetroot
onions
carrots
celery
parsnip
salt and pepper
stock (preferably ham), or water
cabbage (coarsely shredded)
garlic (chopped, or crushed with
   salt) — to taste
tomatoes
sugar
little tomato purée
fresh parsley (chopped)
little plain flour (optional)
soured cream

*5-inch diameter pudding basin
(sufficient for 3 pints liquid), or
small mixing bowl*

Quantities of vegetables should
be used in the following proportions : half beetroot and of
remaining half, one-third onion,
one-third carrot and the last
third equally divided between
celery and parsnip.

Bortsch is the national soup
of the Ukraine, the name
being an old Slav word for
beet. There are numerous
ways of making bortsch but
it always contains root vegetables with a large proportion of beetroot, and
sometimes up to three kinds
of meat.

Method

Cut beetroot, onions, carrots,
celery and parsnip into match-
sticks and pack into the basin
or bowl to fill it.

Lightly season stock or water
and bring to the boil. Turn the
bowl of vegetables into the pan,
cover and simmer for about
20-30 minutes. Coarsely shred
enough cabbage to fill the
bowl, add this with the garlic
to taste. Continue to simmer
gently, uncovered, for a further
20 minutes.

Skin sufficient tomatoes to
half-fill the bowl, squeeze to
remove seeds, then chop flesh
very coarsely. Add to soup,
season well with salt and sugar
and add a little tomato purée
to sharpen the flavour. Simmer
for a further 10 minutes, then
add a handful of chopped
parsley.

The soup can be thickened
lightly with a little flour mixed
with a small quantity of soured
cream. Otherwise serve a bowl
of soured cream separately.

Watchpoint Bortsch should
be slightly piquant in flavour
and not sweet. Add salt and
sugar until this is reached. The
soup should be a thick broth of
vegetables but not too solid.
Dilute if necessary with additional stock.

This bortsch is improved if
made the previous day.

A colourful show of vegetables for making bortsch, a soup that's slightly piquant in taste

Bortschok

2 lb shin of beef
4 pints water
2 onions (1 stuck with a clove)
large bouquet garni
parsley stalks
1 bayleaf
stick of celery
strip of lemon peel
6 peppercorns
salt
3 large cooked beetroots
vinegar, or lemon juice (to taste)
sugar (to taste)
1 can consommé (optional)
$9\frac{1}{2}$-10 fl oz soured cream (optional)

This quantity serves 12 people.

Method

Cut beef into small pieces and put in a large pan with three-quarters of the water ; bring slowly to the boil, removing the scum as it rises, and add the remaining water in two parts. When on boiling point and well skimmed, put in the rest of the ingredients (except the beetroot, consommé and soured cream), partly cover the pan and allow to simmer for about 3 hours.

Strain the broth and return to a clean pan. Grate the beetroot and add to the broth. Cover the pan and leave to infuse on low heat for about 40 minutes. Test for seasoning ; the soup should not taste sweet but have a strong flavour of beetroot. Sharpen with a few drops of vinegar, or lemon juice, salt and sugar. The addition of these last two gives a piquant flavour. Then strain the soup through a piece of muslin. Add the consommé at this stage.

Serve the soup in cups with a bowl of soured cream and the pirozhki handed separately.

Pirozhki

8 oz plain flour
1 teaspoon salt
scant $\frac{1}{2}$ oz yeast
1 teaspoon sugar
3-4 tablespoons milk
2 eggs
2 oz butter

For filling
1 small onion (chopped)
1 oz butter
2 oz mushrooms (sliced) or $\frac{1}{2}$ oz dried mushrooms
2 eggs (hard-boiled and chopped)
3 oz long grain rice (boiled until tender, drained and dried)
salt and pepper
beaten egg (optional) — to bind

Method

Sift the flour with the salt into a warm bowl. Work the yeast with the sugar, then add the milk, warmed to blood heat. Whisk the eggs and add to the flour with the yeast mixture, beating well with your hand. The dough should be rather soft, a little more so than for a scone dough. Then cream the butter, add to the dough and cover the basin with a plate. Leave in the refrigerator overnight ; at the end of this time the dough should have risen to the top of the basin and will be firm enough to handle easily.

To make the filling : soften the onion in a pan with the butter, add the mushrooms and cook briskly for 2-3 minutes ; turn into a bowl and mix with eggs and rice. Season well. If wished, this mixture may be bound with a little beaten egg for easy handling.

Roll out the dough and stamp it out into rounds about 2 ½ inches in diameter : put a spoonful of the filling in the centre of each round, and brush with beaten egg ; bring the edges up over the top and pinch well together. Prove in a warm place for 7-10 minutes and, when lightly risen, fry in deep fat on a rising temperature to allow pies to cook through without overbrowning the surface. If preferred they may be fried some time before they are wanted, then put into a hot oven for 4-5 minutes to heat them through. Alternatively, brush with beaten egg and bake in a hot oven (400°F or Mark 6).

Though these are good baked they are nicer deep fat fried.

Kidney soup

8 oz kidney
2 pints brown stock
bouquet garni
1 oz butter
1 onion (chopped)
1 rounded tablespoon plain flour
1 rounded teaspoon tomato
   purée
salt and pepper
1 wineglass red wine, or golden
   sherry

For liaison (optional)
little arrowroot
1 tablespoon cold water

Method

To prepare kidney, slit the skin on the rounded side and draw it back towards the core. Then pull gently to draw out as much of the core as possible before cutting it off. Cut the kidney open and remove rest of core. Soak in warm, salted water for 1 hour then drain, slice and put into a pan with half the stock and bouquet garni. Cover pan and simmer until kidney is very tender (about 1 hour). Remove bouquet garni and turn soup into a bowl.

Melt butter in the pan, add onion and fry it gently until brown, then stir in flour and tomato purée. Add the remaining stock, season and stir until boiling. Add wine and kidney stock, season and simmer for 10 minutes.

Rub soup through a wire sieve or mix in an electric blender. Reheat in pan and thicken, if necessary, with a little arrowroot slaked in cold water.

Cream of potato soup

1 lb medium-size potatoes
1 onion
1½ oz butter
1 bayleaf
1 pint milk
½ pint water
salt and pepper
1-2 egg yolks
5 tablespoons double cream

Method

Slice potatoes and onion finely. Melt butter in a pan, add vegetables, cover tightly (with greaseproof paper and lid) and cook very slowly for 5-6 minutes. The vegetables must not change colour.

Add bayleaf, milk, water and seasoning. Bring to the boil, cover and simmer for 20-25 minutes until the vegetables are very soft. Take out bayleaf, rub soup through a wire sieve or work in an electric blender. Rinse out pan, add soup, reheat and adjust seasoning.

Mix the egg yolks and cream together in a bowl, add 2-3 tablespoons hot soup to the mixture, then pour back gradually into the soup, whisking well. Stir over heat until very hot but do not boil.

Potage Darblay

1 lb potatoes (peeled and thinly sliced)
1 medium-size onion (thinly sliced)
1½ oz butter
1 pint milk
½ pint water
½ bayleaf
salt and pepper
1 egg yolk
1 teaspoon arrowroot
4 tablespoons single cream

For garnish
1 medium-size carrot
1 medium-size onion
1 stick of celery
1 oz butter
salt and pepper

Method

Melt 1½ oz butter in a pan, add the sliced potatoes and onion and stir. Press a buttered paper on the vegetables, cover with the lid and cook very slowly for 6 minutes. Pour on the milk and water, add bayleaf and seasoning and bring to the boil. Cover pan and simmer for 20 minutes.

Watchpoint Do not put the lid on your pan until you have made quite sure that the soup is only simmering very gently. If your stove is difficult to regulate to a very low heat, it would be wise to leave the lid of the pan lifted at one side, as milk rises in the pan so quickly. If you do have an accident, stop and wipe both pan and stove immediately.

To prepare the garnish : use the red part only of the carrot (not the woody core) and cut this, the onion and celery into julienne strips (for this garnish they should be no longer than 1½ inches). Melt the butter in a small pan, add the vegetables, season lightly and stir. Cover with a buttered paper and a close-fitting lid and cook gently for 8-10 minutes.

Watchpoint The vegetables for the garnish must not colour. As the carrot takes longest to cook, test this with the point of a knife to make sure it is tender. These vegetables can instead be cooked for 3 minutes on top of the stove, then put in a casserole in the oven at 350°F or Mark 4 for 12 minutes or until tender.

Pass the soup through a Mouli sieve or wire sieve, or purée in an electric blender. Return the soup to a clean pan, whisk well to make sure the purée is even and bring to the boil.

To prepare liaison : mix the egg yolk with the arrowroot and cream and add about 2 tablespoons of hot soup to it. Draw the rest of the soup to one side and slowly pour in the liaison, stirring all the time.

Reheat very carefully and slowly so that the soup only just comes to boiling point ; add the garnish and serve.

Julienne strips of carrot, onion and celery are used to garnish the soup

Cream of carrot soup

1 onion
8 oz carrots
1½ oz butter
1½ pints stock
pinch of granulated sugar
salt and pepper
1 small clove of garlic (chopped, or crushed with salt)
¼ pint creamy milk
1 tablespoon cooked long grain rice, or croûtons
1 dessertspoon chopped mint

For liaison (optional)
little arrowroot
1 tablespoon water

Method
Chop onion finely, slice carrots and cook both in 1 oz of butter in a pan for 10 minutes to soften. Add the stock. Simmer for 30-40 minutes, then rub through a sieve or mix in an electric blender. Add sugar and seasoning to taste and garlic. Add milk and reheat soup.

Thicken soup, if necessary, with a little arrowroot slaked in cold water, then whisk in remaining butter. Add rice and mint. Croûtons may be added instead of rice.

Cream of sweetcorn soup

1 small can creamed sweetcorn
1 small can whole kernel sweetcorn (optional)
2 medium-size potatoes
1 medium-size onion
1½ oz butter
1 tablespoon plain flour
1 pint milk
½ pint water
1 bayleaf
salt and pepper

Whole kernel sweetcorn gives soup body, but can be omitted.

Method
Slice the potatoes and onion finely. Melt the butter in a pan, add the potatoes and onion and cook very gently until the vegetables are soft but not coloured. Stir in the flour, and add the milk, water, bayleaf and seasoning. Bring to the boil, stirring well. Add the creamed sweetcorn, simmer gently for 15-20 minutes.

Sieve soup and return to pan with the whole kernel sweetcorn, drained from the liquid. Reheat and adjust seasoning.

Red bean soup

6 oz red beans (soaked overnight
    in water)
1 onion (sliced)
1 carrot (sliced)
2 oz butter
$\frac{1}{2}$ lb tomatoes
1 dessertspoon tomato purée
bouquet garni
$2\frac{1}{2}$-3 pints stock, or water
salt and pepper
Cheddar cheese (grated)

This soup can be used as a
broth, in which case skin the
tomatoes and do not sieve soup.

Red beans can be replaced by
small white haricot beans or
brown Dutch beans.

Red beans can be bought
at most Italian or continental
shops, or from any seedsman
under the name of 'Canadian
Wonder'. They are seeds of a
variety of French bean and have
an especially good flavour.

Method
Drain and rinse beans. Melt
butter in a pan and add onion
and carrot with the beans. Cover
and cook slowly for about 6
minutes.

Halve the unpeeled tomatoes,
remove seeds and strain them.
Add tomato flesh and juice of
seeds to pan. Add tomato purée,
bouquet garni, $2\frac{1}{2}$ pints stock or
water and season. Bring soup
very slowly to the boil and cook
gently for about 2 hours or until
the beans are really tender.

Remove bouquet garni. Rub
soup through a sieve or work
in an electric blender. Rinse
out pan, add soup and reheat.
Add the rest of the stock if it is
too thick. Adjust seasoning and
serve grated cheese separately.

Soup soissonaise
(White bean soup)

$\frac{1}{2}$ lb small white haricot beans
    (soaked overnight in water)
$1\frac{1}{2}$ oz butter
3 onions (thinly sliced)
3 medium-size potatoes (thinly
    sliced)
2 cloves of garlic (crushed with
    salt)
bouquet garni
salt and pepper
about 3 pints light veal, or
    vegetable, stock (include a little
    ham stock if available)
$\frac{1}{4}$ pint creamy milk, or single cream
1 tablespoon freshly chopped
    parsley
croûtons of fried bread

Method
Melt 1 oz of the butter in a pan
and add the onions, potatoes
and garlic ; sweat for a few
minutes. Drain beans and put in
pan with the bouquet garni,
seasoning and two-thirds of the
stock. Bring to the boil, cover
and cook gently over low heat,
or in the oven (set at 325°F or
Mark 3), for about $2\frac{1}{2}$ hours or
until the beans are very tender.
Add more stock during this
time if the liquid is reducing too
quickly.

Rub the soup through a sieve
or work in a blender, rinse out
the pan, return the soup to it,
bring to the boil, adjust
seasoning and beat in the
remaining butter. Add the milk
(or cream) and the chopped
parsley. The soup should be
thick, rich and creamy. Serve
croûtons separately.

Chicken or turkey broth

2 pints strong chicken, or turkey, stock
3 tablespoons carrot (finely diced) — discard centre yellow core
2 tablespoons onion (finely chopped)
2 tablespoons long grain rice
salt and pepper
3 tablespoons double cream
1 dessertspoon chopped parsley

Method
Prepare stock from carcass bones by adding enough water just to cover. For a strong, clear stock, simmer it gently, don't boil hard. Strain and leave to cool ; remove all fat.

Put the stock, vegetables and rice in a pan, season, cover and simmer for 30-40 minutes. Taste for seasoning. Stir in cream, sprinkle with chopped parsley and serve.

Chicken and tomato soup

1 chicken joint (drumstick and thigh), weighing 4-6 oz
1 pint water
1 onion (stuck with a clove)
1 carrot
bouquet garni
salt and pepper
$\frac{1}{4}$-inch thick slice of bread (cut in cubes)
14 oz can tomatoes
2-3 tablespoons double cream

Method
Simmer the chicken joint in the water for 30-40 minutes with the vegetables, bouquet garni, and seasoning to flavour. Take out the chicken, remove the skin and bones, cut the meat into small dice and set on one side.

Remove and discard the bouquet garni and the clove in the onion, add the cubes of bread and tomatoes to the pan and continue to simmer for 15-20 minutes. Rub mixture through a strainer or work in a blender until quite smooth, reheat and taste for seasoning. Add the cream and diced chicken meat just before serving.

Cockie-leekie soup

1 large boiling fowl
4-6 pints cold water
6 leeks
2 tablespoons long grain rice
salt and pepper
1 tablespoon chopped parsley

This traditional Scottish soup is made with an old cock bird, hence its name. This quantity serves 6-8 people.

Method
Place the boiling fowl in a large pot. Add cold water to cover the bird, salt lightly, cover and simmer for 2 hours.

Make a deep, cross-cut in the leeks, wash well and cut into slices. Skim fat off chicken liquid, add leeks and rice and cook gently for a further $1\frac{1}{2}$ hours. Remove the bird and set aside. Skim soup well to remove any fat, taste for seasoning and add the parsley. A slice or two of meat from the leg can be cut into shreds and added to soup before serving.

The chicken may be reheated for another meal with a sauce made from some of the strained broth, used in a curry, or shredded and used cold in a salad or mousse.

Rossolnick

2 sets of turkey, or chicken, giblets (excluding the livers)
1 lb shin of beef
1 tablespoon dripping
2 medium-size onions
$\frac{1}{2}$ teaspoon salt
6-8 peppercorns
bouquet garni
$2\frac{1}{2}$ pints water
kneaded butter (made with 1 oz
$\frac{1}{4}$ butter, $\frac{3}{4}$ oz flour)
salt and pepper
cayenne pepper
$\frac{1}{4}$ pint soured cream
lemon juice (to taste)
1 dill cucumber (shredded)

Method
Wash the giblets thoroughly in salted water, tip them into a colander and pour over half a kettle of boiling water ; drain and cut in rough pieces. Shred the shin of beef. Heat the dripping, add giblets and beef and brown quickly. Then add whole onions, salt, peppercorns and bouquet garni and pour over the cold water. Cover pan and simmer gently for $1\frac{1}{2}$-2 hours.

Strain liquid and reserve the gizzards. Return stock to the pan and thicken with kneaded butter. Season well with salt, pepper and cayenne and beat in the soured cream. Add lemon juice to taste. Cut 2 chicken gizzards, or 1 turkey gizzard, in thin slices, add to the soup and reheat. Sprinkle shredded dill cucumber over the soup ; serve very hot.

Kosher chicken soup

1 boiling chicken (4 lb) with
   giblets (excluding the liver)
salt
2 carrots (peeled)
1 turnip, or parsnip (peeled)
2 onions (peeled)
1 stick of celery
piece of bayleaf
8 peppercorns

Method

Joint the chicken or leave it whole. Place chicken, and salt to season, in a large pan with water to cover. Bring slowly to the boil and skim well. Add vegetables — left whole to avoid clouding the soup — and bayleaf and peppercorns. Simmer on low heat for $1\frac{1}{2}$-2 hours or until the chicken is tender.

Lift the chicken out of the pan (it can be served as the main course of the meal). Strain the liquid and season if necessary. Allow to cool and remove excess fat. Serve soup with one of the following garnishes.

Garnishes

Lockshen

Bring 3-4 pints water and 1 dessertspoon salt to the boil and crumble in 4 oz fine-cut vermicelli. Return to the boil, then simmer for 5 minutes. Drain and rinse ; place in a soup tureen and pour the boiling chicken soup over it.

Kreplech

8 oz plain flour
pinch of salt
2 eggs (beaten)
1 tablespoon oil
2-3 tablespoons water

For filling
1 small onion (very finely
   chopped)
1 tablespoon oil
8 oz cooked meat (minced)
salt and pepper
pinch of ground mace
1 teaspoon chopped parsley
1 egg (beaten)

Many fillings are used for kreplech. An exceptionally good one includes chicken livers, although any type of cooked, minced meat may be used.

Method

First make the filling : soften the onion in the oil with the pan covered. Take off the heat and add the meat, seasoning, mace, parsley and enough beaten egg to bind. Cool before using.

Sift the flour, with a pinch of salt, on to a pastry board. Make a well in the centre and pour in the eggs and oil. Working with the fingers of one hand, begin to draw in the flour and work to a firm dough, adding water as necessary. Knead well until perfectly smooth ; this will take 5-6 minutes. Cover the dough with a cloth and leave it in the refrigerator for 15 minutes.

Roll out the dough quite thinly and cut it into 2-inch squares. Place 1 teaspoon of filling on each square. Dampen the edges of each square and fold over to form a closed triangle, pressing together securely. When the kreplech have been sealed, leave them to dry for about 30 minutes.

Drop kreplech into gently simmering salted water and cook for 15 minutes. Drain and serve in boiling chicken soup.

Kneidlech

5 oz medium matzo meal
salt and pepper
1 tablespoon ground almonds
pinch of ground ginger
8 tablespoons boiling water
1 egg (beaten)
1 tablespoon liquid chicken fat
   (melted from raw chicken fat)

Method
Place matzo meal in a bowl with the seasoning. Sift in the ground almonds and ginger and add the water, egg and chicken fat.

Mix well to a soft dough that may be easily handled. With damp hands roll the dough into balls the size of a walnut and place on a tray or plate. Put this in the refrigerator for 30-60 minutes.

Drop kneidlech balls into boiling salted water and simmer for 6-8 minutes until doubled in size and light. Drain well, pour boiling chicken soup over kneidlech and serve.

Garnishes for chicken soup (from left): kreplech, lockshen, kneidlech

Mushroom soup

$\frac{1}{2}$ lb flat mushrooms
2 medium-size onions (chopped)
1$\frac{1}{2}$ oz butter
2 tablespoons plain flour
2 pints chicken stock
salt and pepper
1 tablespoon long grain rice
1 bayleaf
2 tablespoons chopped watercress

Method

Wash the mushrooms quickly in a bowl of salted water, drain, and cut the stalks level with the mushrooms. Remove the peel. Chop the stalks and peelings finely and slice the mushrooms thinly.

Melt 1 oz of the butter in a pan, add the vegetables, cover with buttered greaseproof paper, pressed well down, and the lid of the pan ; cook them slowly for 5 minutes. Draw pan aside, remove lid and paper, add remaining butter and, when melted, blend in flour and stock. Season, stir until boiling, add the rice and bayleaf. Cover and simmer for 15-20 minutes.

Remove the bayleaf, taste for seasoning, then add the watercress as a garnish just before serving.

Cream of celery soup

1 head of celery (sliced)
1 small onion (finely chopped)
1 pint chicken, or veal, stock
salt and pepper
1 oz butter
1 tablespoon plain flour
$\frac{1}{2}$ pint milk
2 egg yolks (beaten), or 1 teaspoon arrowroot
4-5 tablespoons single cream
croûtons of fried bread

Method
Put celery and onion in a pan with stock. Season and simmer mixture gently for about 20-30 minutes until soft, then pass through a Mouli sieve or mix to a purée in an electric blender. Rinse out pan.

Melt the butter in a large pan, stir in flour off the heat and cook gently until straw-coloured. Blend in milk and celery purée off the heat, return to heat and stir until boiling. Simmer for 2-3 minutes, then taste for seasoning.

Draw pan off heat, add 1-2 teaspoons of hot soup to either egg yolks or arrowroot, mixed with cream, then stir this slowly into soup. Reheat gently until soup has thickened.

Serve croûtons separately.

Croûtons of fried bread are served with cream of celery soup

Cream of artichoke soup

1½ lb jerusalem artichokes (peeled
  and sliced)
3 oz butter
2 medium-size onions (sliced)
1 pint water
salt and pepper
pinch of sugar
1 pint hot milk
2 tablespoons plain flour (mixed
  with 5 tablespoons cold milk)
croûtons of fried bread

Method
Melt the butter in a pan, add the
onion, cover and cook until soft
but not coloured. Now add the
artichokes, cover again and
shake over gentle heat for 10-15
minutes.
 Tip on the water, season, add
sugar, cover and simmer for
15-20 minutes. Rub through a
fine sieve or purée in a blender
and return to the rinsed-out pan
with the hot milk and the mixture
of flour and cold milk. Stir until
boiling, then simmer for a few
minutes. Serve croûtons separately.

Artichoke and tomato soup

1 lb jerusalem artichokes (peeled)
1 small can (8 oz) tomatoes
1 large onion
1 oz butter
1 oz plain flour
1 clove of garlic (crushed with a
  little salt)
pared rind and juice of ½ orange
1 bayleaf
1¼ -1½ pints veal, or chicken, stock
salt and pepper
kneaded butter, or slaked
  arrowroot (optional)
1 small carton (2½ fl oz) single cream,
  or top of milk

Method
Chop onion finely and slice the
artichokes. Soften both these
in a pan with the butter without
colouring, then draw pan aside
and stir in the flour. Add the
tomatoes, garlic, orange rind
tied with the bayleaf, stock and
seasoning. Stir until boiling, then
cover and simmer to about 20
minutes, or until the artichokes
are very tender.
 Remove the bayleaf and
orange rind and put the soup
through a Mouli sieve or work
in a blender. Return to the
rinsed-out pan, adjust seasoning
and thicken if necessary with a
little kneaded butter (or
arrowroot). Reboil, then add
orange juice and cream.

> **Jerusalem artichokes,** not to
> be confused with globe
> artichokes, have a delicate
> but distinctive flavour and
> are particularly suitable for
> soups. They should be
> peeled like potatoes, which
> they resemble except for
> their knobs.

Potage Fréneuse

1 lb young turnips
1 medium-size onion
2 medium-size potatoes
1½ oz butter
1 tablespoon plain flour
2½-3 pints chicken, or vegetable, stock
salt and pepper
2 egg yolks, or 1 teaspoon arrowroot
2½ fl oz single cream
croûtons of fried bread

If using old turnips, ½ lb is sufficient because their flavour is much stronger than that of young ones. After slicing, put them into cold water, bring to the boil and then drain. This will help remove any over-strong taste.

Method

Peel and slice the vegetables and sweat them in the butter in a covered saucepan for 5 minutes (they should not be allowed to colour). Draw the pan aside, stir in the flour and then add the stock. Stir until boiling and then cover the pan and simmer for 35-40 minutes, or until the vegetables are very soft. Work in a blender until very smooth, or rub through a nylon sieve. Return to the rinsed-out pan. Combine the egg yolks (or arrowroot) with the cream, mix with 2-3 tablespoons of the hot soup and add to the pan, stirring over gentle heat until the mixture thickens and is very hot, but not boiling. Adjust the seasoning. Serve croûtons separately.

Cream of asparagus soup

2 bundles of sprue, or 1 bundle of asparagus
1½ pints of veal, or chicken, stock
1 small onion (finely chopped)
1 oz butter
¾ oz plain flour
salt and pepper
2 egg yolks
1 small carton (about 2½ fl oz) double cream

Method

Wash and trim the tied bundle of sprue or asparagus, then cut prepared stalks into 1-inch pieces, reserving a few tips for garnish, and put these in a pan with the stock and onion. Cover pan and simmer until asparagus is tender. Rub the soup through a nylon sieve or work in a blender.

Rinse out the pan. Make a roux with the butter and flour, then add the sieved or blended liquid and season. Bring this to the boil, then simmer it for 2-3 minutes. Add the liaison to the soup and reheat it carefully (do not let it boil). Adjust seasoning, add reserved asparagus tips and serve hot.

Avocado soup

2 avocado pears
1¼ oz butter
1 oz plain flour
1½ pints well-flavoured jellied
   chicken stock
1 shallot, or small onion (finely
   chopped)
1 stick of celery (chopped), or
   ½ teaspoon celery seeds
salt and pepper
2 egg yolks
2-3 tablespoons double cream
pinch of nutmeg

A recipe for cold avocado soup is given on page 73.

Method
Melt the butter, stir in the flour, cook gently until straw-coloured and blend in the stock. Add the shallot (or onion), celery (or seeds) and seasoning and stir until boiling. Cover pan and simmer for 10-15 minutes, then strain liquid.

Peel the avocados, remove the stones, mash flesh with a fork and then press the pulp through a nylon strainer. Add a little of the hot soup to the avocado purée, then put purée into the pan of soup, mix until quite smooth and bring to the boil.

Work the egg yolks and cream in a bowl with a wooden spoon, mix in a little of the hot soup, add mixture to the pan and cook carefully without boiling until the soup thickens. Taste for seasoning, add a pinch of nutmeg and serve.

Pumpkin soup

1½-2 lb pumpkin
3 medium-size potatoes
3 large tomatoes
2 pints water
salt and pepper
1½ tablespoons long grain rice
little milk (optional)
½ oz butter
3 large tablespoons double cream

This is a creamy soup, which is a rich gold in colour.

Method
Peel the pumpkin and cut into chunks. Peel potatoes, wipe and halve tomatoes and remove seeds. Put pumpkin, potatoes and tomatoes into a pan with cold water, season and cook gently for 25-30 minutes until tender.

Boil the rice in salted water until tender (about 12 minutes). Drain and rinse in hot water to separate grains, then set aside. Pass the soup through a sieve or mix in an electric blender. Return to the pan, adjust seasoning and add a little milk if too thick. Reheat, add the rice, butter and cream. Stir well and serve.

Walnut soup

2 oz walnut kernels (preferably
   fresh) ; dried ones should be
   covered with boiling water and
   soaked for 1 hour before using
$\frac{1}{2}$ pint creamy milk
1 oz butter
1 small onion (finely chopped)
1 oz plain flour
1$\frac{1}{2}$ pints strong, well-flavoured
   chicken stock
salt and pepper
2 egg yolks
2$\frac{1}{2}$ fl oz single cream
croûtons of fried bread

This soup can also be served
iced without the addition of
croûtons.

Method
Remove as much skin as possible from the walnut kernels
and grind them through a nut
mill (or a Mouli cheese grater),
or pound well. Scald the milk
and pour it on to the nuts.
Leave to infuse for 30 minutes.

Melt the butter, add onion
and cook until softened but not
coloured. Stir in the flour and,
after a few seconds, pour on
the stock. Blend and bring to
the boil, season and simmer for
7-10 minutes. Add the walnuts
and milk. Mix the egg yolks and
cream together and add a
little of the hot soup to this
liaison before blending it into
the soup. Reheat without boiling, adjust the seasoning and
serve croûtons separately.

Cream of barley soup

2 oz pearl barley (washed and
   soaked overnight in $\frac{1}{2}$ pint water)
2 pints strong veal, or chicken,
   stock (well-seasoned)
1 oz butter
1 rounded tablespoon plain flour
salt and pepper
$\frac{1}{4}$ pint creamy milk
2$\frac{1}{2}$ fl oz single cream

For garnish
1 carrot
1 small turnip
2 rounded tablespoons green peas

Method
Add the barley and water to
the stock, cover and simmer
until barley is tender, about
50-60 minutes. Then strain,
reserving 1-2 tablespoons of
the cooked barley. Rinse out
the pan, melt the butter, stir in
the flour off the heat and cook
gently until straw-coloured. Then
pour on the stock. Bring to the
boil, season and simmer for 5-6
minutes. Add the milk and
cream and the reserved barley.
Continue to simmer while preparing the garnish.

Cut the carrot and turnip into
small dice or, if preferred, make
small 'peas' from the outside of
the turnip and the carrot, using
a vegetable scoop. Cook these
with the green peas until just
tender. Then drain, add to the
soup and serve.

Cream of lettuce soup

2 large lettuces
1 oz butter
1 medium-size onion (finely chopped)
1 rounded tablespoon plain flour
$1\frac{1}{2}$ pints milk
salt and pepper
2 egg yolks, or 1 teaspoon arrowroot
2-3 tablespoons double cream
mint (freshly chopped)
croûtons of fried bread

Any type of lettuce — round or Cos — is suitable for this soup and it is an excellent way to use lettuces that have 'bolted'.

Method

Wash the lettuce thoroughly, then shred it finely. Melt the butter in a pan, add the lettuce and onion, cover with a buttered paper and the lid of the pan and cook very gently for 8-10 minutes. Remove pan from heat and stir in the flour. Scald the milk, blend with the lettuce mixture and season ; stir until boiling, then leave to simmer very gently, with the lid half off the pan, for 10-15 minutes. Pass liquid through a Mouli sieve or work in a blender.

Return liquid to the rinsed-out pan, reheat to boiling point before adding liaison.

If using egg for the liaison, work the yolks and cream together with a wooden spoon and add 2 tablespoons of the hot soup ; return this mixture very slowly (in a thin steady stream) to the pan of soup and reheat carefully, without boiling. If using the arrowroot mixed with cream, stir it briskly into the hot soup and reboil. Taste for seasoning.

Pour soup into a hot tureen and sprinkle with the chopped mint. Serve the fried croûtons separately.

Cream of spinach soup

$1\frac{1}{2}$ lb spinach
$1\frac{1}{4}$ oz butter
1 shallot (finely chopped)
1 oz plain flour
1 pint chicken, or vegetable, stock
salt and pepper
$\frac{1}{2}$ pint milk
little grated nutmeg
2-3 tablespoons double cream

For garnish
croûtons of fried bread, or lightly
    whipped cream and lemon
    slices, or hard-boiled egg
    (quartered)

1 *Removing stalks from spinach*
2 *Sieving the cooked spinach*

Method
Pick over the spinach, remove
the stalks and wash thoroughly
in several changes of water.
Cook it for 3 minutes in boiling
salted water to set the colour.
Drain and then press spinach
between two plates to remove
as much water as possible.

Melt the butter, add the
shallot and cook for 2-3 minutes until soft, but not coloured.
Blend in the flour and continue
cooking until the colour of straw.
Tip on the stock, add the
spinach, season and stir until
boiling ; cover and simmer for
20 minutes. Rub through a fine
nylon sieve or purée in a blender.
Return the soup to the saucepan
and then add the milk to give a
creamy consistency ; taste for
seasoning and add a small
pinch of nutmeg.

If serving in a hot tureen, stir
in the cream while soup is in the
saucepan and reheat without
boiling. Hand croûtons separately. If serving directly in
soup cups, put a spoonful of
lightly whipped cream and a
slice of lemon in each cup after
filling, or serve a quarter of
hardboiled egg. with each one.

Cream of spinach soup may be served in soup cups and garnished with whipped cream and a slice of lemon. Alternatively serve it with croûtons, or quarters of hard-boiled egg

Potage vert

1 bunch of spring onions
$\frac{1}{2}$ bunch of watercress
$\frac{1}{2}$ lb spinach
3-4 sprays of parsley
1 pint chicken stock
1 pint ham stock
salt and pepper
1 rounded tablespoon cornflour
3-4 fl oz double cream
squeeze of lemon juice

Method

Wash, trim and finely chop the spring onions, watercress, spinach and parsley. Mix chicken and ham stock, bring to the boil and add the chopped vegetables. Season with pepper and simmer gently for 15-20 minutes. Rub mixture through a fine strainer, or purée in a blender, and return the soup to the rinsed-out pan.

Mix the cornflour to a smooth paste with the cream, add to the soup and stir until it is boiling. Simmer soup for 3-5 minutes, taste for seasoning, then sharpen with a squeeze of lemon juice. Serve at once.

Potage crème de fromage

1 large Spanish onion (finely chopped)
$1\frac{1}{2}$-2 oz butter
2 oz plain flour
$1\frac{3}{4}$ pints milk (infused with a bayleaf, 6 peppercorns and a blade of mace)
salt and pepper
point of cayenne pepper, or a dash of Tabasco sauce
2 egg yolks
$2\frac{1}{2}$ fl oz double cream
$1\frac{1}{2}$-2 oz Cheshire cheese (finely grated)
2-3 tablespoons cooked peas
potato croûtons

Method

Put the onion into a pan, cover with cold water and bring to the boil, then drain, rinse and drain again. Melt 1 oz of the butter in a pan, add the onion, cover and cook slowly for about 5 minutes without allowing to colour.

To make cheese soup, egg yolk and cream liaison and grated cheese are stirred into flavoured milk mixture

Draw aside. Add the rest of the butter, then stir in the flour. The mixture should be soft and fairly liquid.

Blend in the flavoured milk, season with salt, pepper and cayenne (or Tabasco) and stir until boiling. Simmer for 6-7 minutes, or until delicately flavoured, and strain through a fine strainer. Return soup to the rinsed-out pan. Put the egg yolks into a basin, mix with the cream, add 2-3 tablespoons of hot soup and gradually stir this into the soup, also adding the grated cheese. Reheat carefully, stirring all the time, until thoroughly hot, but do not boil.

Serve this soup with 2-3 tablespoons cooked peas stirred in, and hand a dish of potato croûtons.

The cheese soup is shown here garnished with cheese profiteroles (if preferred, serve potato croûtons)

Cream of chestnut soup

1 lb fresh, or $\frac{1}{2}$ lb dried, chestnuts
1$\frac{1}{2}$ pints chicken, or veal, stock
2 oz butter
1 medium-size onion (finely chopped)
3 sticks of celery (chopped)
salt and pepper
kneaded butter (optional)
1 small carton (about 2$\frac{1}{2}$ fl oz) single cream
croûtons of fried bread

Method

First prepare the chestnuts : put fresh ones in a pan of cold water, bring to the boil and, once the water is bubbling, take pan off heat. Lift chestnuts out of the water with a draining spoon. Hold each one in a cloth while you strip off the outer and inner skins with a small, sharp knife. If the skin doesn't come away easily, put the nut back into the hot water for 1 minute. Place the skinned nuts in a pan with enough of the stock to cover and 1 oz butter and cook for about 1 hour, or until they are soft. Rub the chestnuts through a sieve, or purée in a blender.

If you use dried chestnuts, first soak them in cold water overnight. Then drain and put them in a pan with enough stock to cover and 1 oz butter and cook them for about 20 minutes, or until they are tender. Then rub them through a sieve, or work in a blender, and use as in the rest of the method.

Melt the remaining butter, add the onion, cover pan and cook until the onion is soft but not coloured. Then blend in remaining stock, celery and chestnut purée ; season to taste. Stir until boiling, simmer soup for 20 minutes. Thicken, if necessary, with kneaded butter and taste again for seasoning.

Put the cream into a hot soup tureen and then pour over the boiling soup through a strainer. Stir well and serve the croûtons separately.

A soup made from chestnuts, or walnuts (see page 60), — is an unusual starter

Cold soups

Chilled and iced soups make unusual but delicious starters for summer meals. On a really hot day, your guests will have to be tempted into eating, and a refreshing, cold soup will certainly whet their appetites.

There is no rule about soups that can or cannot be served cold. A certain winner is a chilled bisque, rich with the flavour of shellfish and velvety smooth in texture. And for a truly summery soup try one made from cucumber or avocado.

A saving grace of chilled soups is that most of them can also be served hot — so if the weather turns cold at the last minute, and you have nothing more cheering to offer than salads and iced desserts, heat up your cold soup and warm the mood of your guests that way ! But for the 'set fair' days, when a Mediterranean touch is called for, try a Spanish gazpacho served with the ice cubes in the soup. This is a recipe you don't even have to cook, so you can stay cool in the kitchen too.

Lebanese cucumber soup

1 cucumber
salt and pepper
$\frac{3}{4}$ pint strong chicken stock
$\frac{1}{4}$ pint tomato juice
2 cartons (5 fl oz each) of yoghourt
  (unsweetened)
$\frac{1}{4}$ pint single cream
2 oz shelled prawns (fresh, or
  frozen) — coarsely chopped
1 clove of garlic

To garnish
1 tablespoon chopped mint
1 hard-boiled egg (chopped)

Method

Peel and dice the cucumber, salt it lightly and leave on a plate for 30 minutes before draining.

Meanwhile mix the stock, tomato juice and yoghourt together; when quite smooth add drained cucumber and cream, seasoning and the prawns. Chill for 2-3 hours.

Rub a soup tureen or bowls with the garlic. Pour in the soup and sprinkle with the chopped mint and hard-boiled egg just before serving.

Lebanese cucumber soup makes a refreshing start to a summer meal

Iced cucumber soup

2 medium-size cucumbers
2 shallots, or 1 medium-size
  onion (finely chopped)
3 pints chicken stock
2 oz butter
2 tablespoons plain flour
salt and pepper
3 egg yolks
6-8 tablespoons double cream
2-3 drops of green edible colouring

To garnish
1 tablespoon finely chopped mint,
  or chives
3 tablespoons double cream
  (very lightly whipped)

This quantity serves 8 people.

Method

Peel cucumbers and cut into $\frac{1}{2}$ inch slices ; simmer in a pan with shallot and stock for 15-20 minutes, until soft. Rub through a nylon strainer or work in a blender until smooth. Melt the butter, add the flour off the heat and cook until straw-coloured and marbled in appearance. Blend in the cucumber liquid, stir until boiling, then season and simmer for 2-3 minutes.

Work the yolks and cream together in a bowl with a wooden spoon, draw the soup off the heat and then very slowly add about 3-4 tablespoons of the hot soup to this liaison. Return this to the saucepan a little at a time, then reheat gently without boiling until the soup has thickened. Colour the soup very delicately, adjust seasoning, and pour into a container ready for chilling. Cover soup to prevent a skin forming and when cold place it in refrigerator or in a bowl packed with ice to chill.

Remember to chill the tureen and soup cups before serving. Put a rounded teaspoon of lightly whipped cream in each cup, or the equivalent in a tureen, and stir it in gently to give the soup a streaky look ; sprinkle with mint or chives.

Left : adding some of the hot soup to the liaison of egg yolks and cream
Right : to make a chilled soup really attractive, serve it in individual cups set in a plate of ice

Potage crème d'or

1 medium-size onion
1½ oz butter
1 can carrots (medium, or large)
2 pints chicken stock, or canned consommé
1 small can frozen orange juice
salt and pepper
scant ½ pint double cream
snipped chives

Method

Chop the onion finely. Melt the butter in a small pan, add the onion and cook slowly until soft but not coloured. Drain the carrots and put in a blender or press through a nylon sieve with the onion ; mix purée with the stock (or consommé), orange juice, seasoning and cream and stir gently to blend. Adjust the seasoning and add the chives. Chill before serving.

This soup can be served hot. **Watchpoint** If the soup is served hot, be careful not to let it boil after the orange juice and cream have been added, otherwise the orange flavour is lost.

Vichyssoise

the white part of 3 large leeks
1 stick of celery
2 potatoes (weighing 4-6 oz in all)
1 oz butter
2 pints jellied chicken stock
salt and pepper
$\frac{1}{4}$ pint double cream
1 tablespoon snipped chives

This is the classic iced soup of American origin, and must be made with jellied chicken stock and cream. In this country it is not always possible to find leeks in summer, but a mild-flavoured onion such as a Spanish onion can be used instead.

Method
Slice the leeks, celery and potatoes finely and sweat vegetables in butter until just soft without allowing them to colour.
Watchpoint While sweating the vegetables, press a piece of damp greaseproof paper right down on top of them under the lid of the pan. Stir occasionally to avoid all danger of browning.

Blend in the stock, bring to the boil, season and simmer for 12-15 minutes. Rub through a Mouli sieve or work in an electric blender. Taste for seasoning and stir in the cream. Leave soup until cold then whisk for a few seconds and chill.

Sprinkle chives on the top of each serving. The soup should have the consistency of cream, and be smooth and bland.

Avocado soup

2 avocado pears
$\frac{3}{4}$ pint strong, well-flavoured chicken stock (free from grease)
$\frac{1}{4}$ pint double cream (lightly whipped)
$\frac{1}{2}$ pint plain yoghourt
$\frac{1}{2}$ teaspoon grated onion
1 bottle of tomato cocktail, or tomato juice (about $\frac{1}{4}$ pint)
salt and pepper
dash of Tabasco sauce

A recipe for hot avocado soup is given on page 59.

Method
Peel the avocado pears, remove the stones and mash flesh with a fork until smooth. Whisk in the chicken stock, cream, yoghourt, onion and tomato juice. Season well, adding a dash of Tabasco. If the consistency of the soup is too thick, dilute with a little more stock. Turn soup into a bowl and chill well.

Crème normande

1 large mild onion (chopped)
1 oz butter
1 tablespoon curry powder
2 dessert apples
1 dessertspoon plain flour
1½ pints chicken stock
1 dessertspoon cornflour
¼ pint double cream
2 eggs yolks
salt and pepper
lemon juice
watercress (to garnish)

Method

Soften the onion in the butter without colouring. Add curry powder and one apple, peeled, cored and sliced. After a few minutes stir in the flour. Cook for 1 minute, then pour on the stock and add the cornflour, first slaking it with a little of the stock. Bring to the boil and simmer for 5 minutes, then add cream mixed with the egg yolks. Reheat to thicken without boiling, then put the soup through a fine sieve or blender. Season and chill.

Peel and dice the remaining apple, mix with a little lemon juice and add to the soup just before serving. Garnish with watercress.

Iced curry soup

1 oz butter
4 shallots, or 1 medium-size onion (finely chopped)
1 tablespoon curry paste
1 oz plain flour
1¾ pints chicken, or well-flavoured vegetable, stock
strip of lemon rind
1 bayleaf
¼ pint boiling water
1 tablespoon ground almonds
1 tablespoon desiccated coconut
1 dessertspoon arrowroot
1 tablespoon cold stock, or water

For cream topping
1 glass port
1 teaspoon curry powder
1 dessertspoon apricot jam
4 tablespoons double cream

Method

Melt three-quarters of the butter, add the shallot (or onion) and cook it slowly until just turning colour, then add the curry paste and a dusting of the flour ; fry gently for 4-5 minutes. Stir in the remainder of the butter and when it has melted blend in the rest of the flour and the stock ; bring to the boil. Add the lemon rind and bayleaf and simmer for 20 minutes. Strain the liquid and return it to the rinsed pan ; continue simmering for 10-15 minutes.

Meanwhile pour the boiling water over the almonds and coconut and leave them to soak for 30 minutes, then squeeze mixture in a piece of muslin and add the 'milk' obtained to the soup. Mix the arrowroot with the tablespoon of cold stock (or water), add it to the pan and reboil. Strain soup again, allow it to cool and then chill.

To make the cream topping ; mix the port and curry powder together and simmer until reduced to half quantity. Leave this until cold, then mix in the jam and squeeze the mixture in a piece of muslin ; reserve the liquid. Lightly whip the cream and stir in the 'essence' from the wine and curry mixture. Serve the soup with a spoonful of this cream in each soup cup.

Iced curry soup is an ideal summer starter, served in individual cups with a spoonful of cream topping in each

Almond and grape soup

2 oz almonds
½ pint milk
1 small onion (finely sliced)
1½ oz butter
2 good tablespoons plain flour
1½ pints strong chicken stock
salt and pepper
2 sticks of celery (sliced)
2 egg yolks
2-3 tablespoons double cream
1 tablespoon chopped parsley
6 oz white grapes (to garnish)

Method

Blanch and finely chop the almonds. Scald the milk, add the nuts, cover the pan and leave to infuse. Slowly cook the onion in butter until soft but not coloured. Blend in the flour and chicken stock, season and stir until boiling. Add the celery to the pan and simmer gently for 15 minutes.

Emulsify the almonds and milk in an electric blender or pass them through a fine nylon sieve. Strain the chicken broth and add it to the almond mixture. Reheat the soup and adjust the seasoning. Mix the egg yolks with the cream, add 2-3 tablespoons of the hot soup, then slowly stir this liaison into the soup. Then chill. Serve sprinkled with parsley, with a few peeled and pipped grapes in each soup cup.

Hollandaise soup

2 pints strong chicken stock
salt and pepper
2 oz butter
2 oz plain flour
scant 4 fl oz single cream
2 egg yolks

For garnish
2 tablespoons shelled peas
1 rounded tablespoon carrot 'peas' (scooped out from the red part of a carrot with a vegetable scoop)
1 rounded tablespoon turnip 'peas'

Method

Season stock and remove any grease. Melt the butter in a large pan, stir in flour off heat and cook for a few seconds. Pour on stock, blend and stir until boiling. Simmer for 10 minutes.

Meanwhile prepare and cook garnish in boiling salted water. Blend cream and egg yolks together and mix with 2-3 tablespoons of the hot soup, to make liaison. Skim soup, if necessary, and add liaison. Adjust seasoning and add drained garnish. Thicken the soup over heat without boiling, then chill.

Gazpacho

1 cup (3 oz) breadcrumbs
red wine vinegar
2 cloves of garlic
salt and pepper
2 small ridge, or greenhouse,
  cucumbers
1 onion
1 green pepper
$\frac{1}{4}$ pint salad oil
2 lb tomatoes (rubbed through
  a sieve)
iced water

For serving
croûtons (made from toast)
bowl of ice cubes

Method
Soak the crumbs in 2 table-spoons vinegar. Pound the garlic to a cream with 1 teaspoon of salt. Roughly chop one cucumber, the onion and half the green pepper and put them, with the crumbs, into a mortar. Pound to a paste, then rub the paste through a fine sieve. Add the oil, a few drops at a time, as for mayonnaise. Taste soup and season with a little more vinegar, if necessary, and pour into a tureen.

Add the tomato pulp and some iced water. The amount of water depends on the juiciness of the tomatoes, but the soup should have a fairly thin consistency. Season and chill well.

The remaining cucumber and pepper, diced, may be added to the soup after chilling or served separately. Small croûtons and a bowl of ice cubes should be handed separately (in Spain, ice cubes are added to this traditional soup before it is drunk).

Chilled prawn bisque

6 oz shelled prawns (chopped)
1 onion (finely chopped)
1 oz butter
2 lb tomatoes, or 1 medium-size
  can (1 lb 14 oz) tomatoes
3 caps of canned pimiento
  (chopped)
1 dessertspoon tomato purée
2-2$\frac{1}{2}$ pints chicken stock
arrowroot
$\frac{1}{4}$ pint double cream

This soup can also be served hot.

Method
Cook the onion in the butter until softened, then add the tomatoes (skinned, cut in half and squeezed to remove the seeds). Cover the pan and slowly cook the vegetables to a pulp. Add the pimiento, tomato purée and stock. Simmer for 10-15 minutes. Then add the prawns and work in an electric blender. Thicken the soup lightly with arrowroot (mixed with a little water) and chill.
Note : if a blender is not used, pass the vegetables and liquid through a fine sieve and add the prawns, finely chopped, after the soup has been thickened.

Whip the cream and stir it into the soup just before serving.

Greek lemon soup (Avgolemono)

thinly pared rind and juice of 1
   small lemon
good oz butter
3 shallots (finely chopped)
1 rounded tablespoon plain flour
2 pints jellied chicken stock
2-3 egg yolks
3-4 tablespoons double cream
   (lightly whipped)

For garnish
1 egg white
1-2 tablespoons cream, or top of
   the milk
salt and pepper

Method
Melt butter in a pan, add chopped shallots, cover and cook very slowly for 2-3 minutes, but do not allow them to colour. Draw pan aside, stir in the flour, blend in the stock and bring to the boil. Simmer for 10 minutes, then add the thinly pared rind of the lemon and the strained juice.

Watchpoint Care must be taken that this soup is not too sharp in flavour. To prevent this, add the lemon juice to taste.

Continue to simmer the soup for a further 7-10 minutes. Then strain liquid, return to the rinsed-out pan and draw aside.

Meanwhile set the oven at 325°F or Mark 3. Lightly beat the egg white with a fork just to break it, add the cream (or milk) with the seasoning. Turn this mixture into an individual soufflé dish or cocotte. Bake in pre-set oven for 7-10 minutes, or until firm to the touch, leave until cold and turn out, slice and cut out into tiny rounds, or diamonds.

Mix the egg yolks together, add a little of the warm soup, then add this mixture to the soup as for a liaison. Reheat, stirring constantly, but do not allow to boil. Leave soup to cool, then put in the refrigerator to chill. Add the lightly whipped cream and the egg white garnish just before serving.

Hot starters

A delicious opening to a well cooked meal, a starter serves a double function. It's a dish in itself — and as such is worthy of more than the cursory attention given to it by many cooks ; and it's also a herald of things to come, an appetiser for the main course.

Don't spoil a meal by spending hours on the main dish and then slapping half a grapefruit in front of everyone as the easiest way of paying tribute to the convention of a three-course meal. There is an undoubted place for a well prepared half grapefruit as a starter (see page 137) — but there is also room for a variety of other things.

The first course should complement the rest of the meal. So, if you are serving a main course of curry, you don't serve a spicy first course ; if your main course is to be rich and substantial, your first course should be slight and tasty ; a light salad main course will follow well from a filling fish dish or pasta.

In cool weather guests will appreciate a hot starter. Apart from the flavour of the dish itself, a hot starter gives an immediate air of festivity to the meal, for it at once signifies that you have taken trouble to please ! Not, of course, that a hot starter is necessarily any more effort to prepare than a cold one — it just looks that way.

Scallops with red wine and mushrooms

4 large scallops
¼ pint water
2-3 drops of lemon juice
1 oz butter
1 medium-size onion (finely chopped)
3 oz button mushrooms (quartered)
1 clove of garlic (crushed with salt)
1 rounded dessertspoon plain flour
1 wineglass of fish, or vegetable, stock, or liquor from scallops
1 teaspoon tomato purée
salt
black pepper (ground from mill)
1 wineglass red wine
2 tomatoes
4 tablespoons browned breadcrumbs
2 oz butter (melted)
creamed potatoes (optional)
parsley (chopped)

Method

Remove scallops from shells, wash and dry them well.

Put scallops into a shallow pan, pour on the water and add lemon juice. Cover and poach for 5 minutes. Turn into a basin, reserving liquid. Melt butter in the pan, add onion, cover and cook gently for 2 minutes. Put in mushrooms, increase heat and cook briskly for a further 2 minutes, stirring all the time. Draw pan aside, stir in garlic and flour and blend ; add the stock or liquor from the scallops, tomato purée and seasoning. Bring to the boil and simmer for 2-3 minutes.

Boil wine in a small pan until reduced by about a third. Add to the sauce and simmer for a further 5 minutes.

Scald and skin tomatoes, quarter and remove the seeds and cut away the little piece of hard stalk. Cut each piece of tomato in half lengthways and add to the sauce with the scallops. Spoon at once into the deep shells. Sprinkle well with the breadcrumbs tossed in melted butter.

If using creamed potato, pipe it round the shells to make a thick border before setting them on a baking sheet.

Put scallops in oven pre-set at 375°F or Mark 5 for about 5 minutes, until they are brown. Dust with chopped parsley before serving.

Coquilles St. Jacques armoricaine

5-6 good-size scallops
4-6 peppercorns
squeeze of lemon juice
1 bayleaf
1 medium-large carrot (finely
    diced)
2-3 sticks of celery (finely diced)
1 large, or 2 small, leeks (finely
    sliced)
1 oz butter
2-3 brussels sprouts (finely sliced)
    — optional
2 tablespoons white wine, or water,
    or 1-2 tomatoes (scalded, skinned,
    seeds removed)
1-2 tablespoons grated Cheddar,
    or Gruyère, cheese

For cream sauce
½ oz butter
½ oz plain flour
7½ fl oz creamy milk
salt and pepper

4-5 scallop shells

Method

Wash and clean the scallops and put them into a pan. Cover with cold water, add the peppercorns, lemon juice and bayleaf and bring to the boil ; poach for 5-7 minutes.

Set the oven at 350°F or Mark 4. To prepare the mirepoix : put carrot, celery and leek in a flameproof casserole with butter ; cover and cook on a low heat for 3-4 minutes. Add the brussels sprouts (if using) and the white wine (or water, or tomatoes). Cover and put in oven for 5-6 minutes.

Put a spoonful of the mirepoix into each scallop shell. Drain the scallops, slice them into rounds and lay these on top of the mirepoix. Make sauce as for a béchamel, adding any juice from the mirepoix, and spoon a little over the contents of each shell. Sprinkle with the cheese and brown under the grill or in the oven set at 450°F or Mark 8.

Sole Georgette

1 filleted sole (weighing 1½ lb)
4 large long-shaped potatoes
1 wineglass white wine
½ wineglass water
slice of onion
6 peppercorns
1¾ oz butter
1 rounded tablespoon plain flour
salt and pepper
5 tablespoons top of milk
¼ pint milk
4 oz prawns (shelled)
grated cheese (to sprinkle)

Forcing bag and large rose pipe

Method

Set the oven at 375°F or Mark 5.

Scrub the potatoes well, dry and roll them in salt. Bake until tender (about 1½-2 hours).

Wash and dry the fillets ; fold them over to the length of the potatoes. Place fillets in an ovenproof dish, pour over the wine and water, add the onion and peppercorns. Poach in a slow to moderate oven (325-350°F or Mark 3-4) for 10-12 minutes.

Melt ¾ oz butter in a saucepan, stir in the flour off the heat and strain on the liquid from the fish. Season. Blend and stir until boiling. Add the top of the milk, adjust seasoning. Add 1-2 tablespoons of the sauce to the prawns to bind them.

When potatoes are soft, cut off the tops lengthways, scoop out the pulp, divide the prawn mixture evenly between the potatoes and place inside the skins. Lay a fillet of sole on top and coat with the rest of the sauce. Mash or sieve the scooped-out potato and beat in enough hot milk (2-4 fl oz), some butter (about 1 oz), and seasoning to give a purée to pipe round the edge of each potato skin ; sprinkle with grated cheese and bake until brown in a quick oven (400°F or Mark 6). Alternatively, replace the 'lid' and reheat for a few minutes in the oven.

Serve each potato very hot in a napkin.

1 *Scooping out cooked potato from the skin to make container for fish ; alongside are the prawns mixed with a little of the sauce*
2 *Piping potato purée round potato skin after it has been filled*

Sole meunière aux moules

6 fillets of sole, or 1 sole (weighing 2 lb filleted)
1 quart mussels
bouquet garni
1 stick of celery
1 wineglass water
3-4 oz unsalted butter
seasoned flour
juice and grated rind of $\frac{1}{2}$ lemon
1 tablespoon parsley
pepper (ground from mill)
quarters of lemon (to garnish)

Method

Skin the fillets and, if using from whole sole, cut each one in half diagonally. Wash and dry them, and set aside.

Wash and scrape the mussels thoroughly and put into a roomy saucepan with the bouquet garni and stick of celery. Pour over a wineglass of water. Cover the pan and bring slowly to the boil, shaking occasionally. (The mussels will open as they cook.)

Take up the mussels, shell them and pull off the beards. Set the mussels aside in a little melted butter and keep warm.

Flour the fillets, heat a large thick frying pan and melt about 1 oz of the butter. When foaming, lay in the fillets, skinned side downwards. Cook fairly briskly for 3-4 minutes or until golden-brown and then turn over carefully and continue to fry on the other side.

Lift out the fillets on to a serving dish and overlap them down it (do not drain on paper). Put dish in the oven to keep warm.

To serve, wipe out the pan, reheat and drop in the remaining butter with the lemon rind. Cook until just turning colour, then add the lemon juice, mussels, parsley and pepper. Shake over the heat for a few seconds and then pour over the sole. Serve very hot with quarters of lemon, either arranged around the dish or handed separately.

1 Arranging fried fillets of sole overlapping on a serving dish
2 Pouring mussels, lemon, parsley and pepper mixture over soles

Sole and mussels are cooked in butter, and served with quarters of lemon

Fish croquettes vert-pré

1 lb fresh haddock fillet
salt and pepper
6 peppercorns
squeeze of lemon juice
2 tablespoons water
$\frac{1}{2}$ lb potatoes
1 bunch of watercress
1 oz butter
1 egg
fried parsley (to garnish)

For coating croquettes
2 tablespoons seasoned flour
1 egg (beaten)
dried white breadcrumbs

Deep fat bath

Method

Set oven at 350°F or Mark 4. Wash the haddock, then place in a lightly buttered ovenproof dish. Season with salt, add the peppercorns, lemon juice and water. Cover with a buttered paper and poach fish in pre-set oven for 12-15 minutes. Drain fish, then flake and crush with a fork.

Peel and quarter the potatoes ; wash the watercress well ; cook both together in a pan of boiling, salted water until the potatoes are just tender. Drain well, dry both over gentle heat, then pass through a sieve.

Mix the fish and potato and watercress purée together, add the butter, season to taste, add egg and beat well. Form mixture into croquettes, using a palette knife to shape the ends. Roll the croquettes in seasoned flour, coat with beaten egg and white crumbs. Fry croquettes in deep fat until golden-brown (about 3 minutes) then drain on absorbent paper. Serve garnished with fried parsley and hand tartare sauce separately.

Cod Cubat

1¼-2 lb cod fillet
salt and pepper
juice of ½ small lemon
8 oz flat mushrooms
¼ oz butter
1 dessertspoon chopped mixed
　herbs
pinch of ground mace

For thick béchamel sauce
1 oz butter
2 tablespoons plain flour
½ pint flavoured milk (infused
　with 3 peppercorns, ½ bayleaf,
　1 blade of mace)
salt and pepper

For mornay sauce
¾ oz butter
1 rounded tablespoon plain flour
½ pint milk
1½ oz cheese (grated) — Cheddar,
　or half Parmesan, half Gruyère
salt and pepper

To finish
1 teaspoon grated Parmesan
　cheese
1 French roll (for croûtes)
oil, or butter (for frying)

Method
Set the oven at 275°F or Mark 1.
Fillet the fish, remove the skin,
then cut each piece in three.
Buying and preparing the fish
in this way gives the best-shaped
portion of fish to serve between
two sauces.

Place the fish in a well-
buttered ovenproof dish, season
and sprinkle with lemon juice ;
cover with buttered paper and
cook in pre-set oven for 15 minutes.

Prepare béchamel sauce.

Wash and finely chop the
mushrooms, without removing
peel or stalks, and sauté in
butter, until dry ; add seasoning, herbs and mace, mix with
the béchamel sauce and set
pan aside.

Prepare the mornay sauce
as for a béchamel, then draw
aside, beat in the cheese and
season to taste.

Reheat the mushroom mixture
and spread down the centre of
the serving dish, arrange the
fish on top and coat with the
mornay sauce. Sprinkle with
Parmesan cheese and brown
under grill just before serving.

Slice the roll and fry in the oil
and butter until golden-brown.
Garnish dish with these croûtes.
Watchpoint If this dish is to be
baked ahead of time and
reheated, mix a dessertspoon of
browned crumbs with the cheese
sprinkled on top to prevent pools
of grease forming.

*Placing the cooked cod on mush-
room mixture in the serving dish* 87

Prawn pilaf

8 oz long grain rice
pinch of saffron
1 onion
2 oz butter
salt and pepper
1¼-1½ pints chicken stock, or stock
  made from bouillon cubes
2 tablespoons grated Parmesan
  cheese

For prawn salpicon
8 oz prawns (shelled)
1 oz butter
1 shallot (finely chopped)
8 oz tomatoes
1 teaspoon paprika pepper
1 teaspoon tomato purée
salt
pepper (ground from mill)
pinch of granulated sugar
few whole prawns (to garnish)
  — optional

*7-inch diameter border, or ring,
mould(1¼-pints capacity)*

Method
Set the oven at 375°F or Mark 5
and butter the border or ring
mould. Soak saffron in an egg
cup of boiling water for 30 minutes.

Slice the onion finely, put into
a flameproof casserole with
two-thirds of the butter, cover
and cook slowly until soft but
not coloured. Add the rice and
fry for 2-3 minutes until it looks
almost transparent. Then add the
saffron and its liquid, seasoning
and 1¼ pints of stock. Bring to
the boil, stir once with a fork,
put in the oven and cook for
20-30 minutes or until rice is
tender and the stock absorbed.
Look at the rice after 20 minutes
and if it is not quite tender but
all the stock has been absorbed,
add the extra ¼ pint of chicken
stock.

When rice is cooked remove
from oven, dot the remaining
butter over the top, dust with the
cheese, cover and leave to
absorb these for 5-10 minutes.

Meanwhile prepare the
salpicon. Melt the butter in a pan,
add chopped shallot, cover and
cook slowly until soft. Scald,
skin and quarter the tomatoes
and scoop out the seeds ; rub
seeds in a strainer and keep the
juice. Add paprika to the shallot,
cook for 1 minute, then stir in
the tomato purée and juice from
the seeds. Season and add a
pinch of sugar. Simmer for 2-3
minutes. Add shelled prawns
and tomatoes to the pan and
toss well over the heat.

Stir the topping of butter and
cheese into the rice with a fork
and then spoon pilaf carefully
into the buttered border or ring
mould ; press lightly, turn on to
a hot serving dish and spoon the
prawn salpicon into the centre of
the pilaf. Garnish with whole
prawns if wished.

*Spooning the prawn salpicon
mixture into the centre of the pilaf*

Trout à la genevoise

5-6 small, even-size trout
salt
1 wineglass water
4-6 peppercorns
1½ lb potatoes (cut into small
   balls and plainly boiled)

For sauce
1 small onion (finely chopped)
1 small carrot (finely chopped)
1 oz butter
2 wineglasses red wine
kneaded butter (made with ¾ oz
   butter and ½ oz plain flour)
salt and pepper
a dash of anchovy essence
a little thyme (chopped)
1 dessertspoon chopped parsley

Method
Set the oven at 350°F or Mark 4 and clean and trim the trout. Butter an ovenproof dish well, lay in the trout and add a little salt, the water and peppercorns. Cover with a buttered paper and poach for about 15 minutes in pre-set oven.

To make the sauce : sauté the onion and carrot in ½ oz of the butter, then add the wine and simmer until reduced to half quantity. Strain off the liquor from the trout and add to the pan. Simmer for 4-5 minutes, thicken slightly with kneaded butter, reboil, adjust seasoning and add the anchovy essence, thyme, remaining butter and chopped parsley. Spoon sauce over trout ; serve potato balls at each end of dish.

Salmon steaks aux gourmets

3 salmon steaks (each weighing
  6-8 oz)
1 wineglass white wine
squeeze of lemon juice
1 slice of onion
6 peppercorns
sprig of parsley

For hollandaise sauce
4 tablespoons tarragon vinegar
1 blade of mace
6 peppercorns
3 egg yolks (beaten)
4-6 oz butter
tomato purée
grated rind of ½ orange

For garnish
3 tomatoes
3 oz button mushrooms
½ oz butter
squeeze of lemon juice
salt and pepper

This quantity serves 6 people.

Method

Wash and dry salmon steaks. Set oven at 350°F or Mark 4. Place steaks in an ovenproof dish and poach them in the white wine and lemon juice, with onion and seasonings, in pre-set oven for about 15 minutes.

To prepare hollandaise sauce : boil tarragon vinegar with the mace and peppercorns to reduce to a scant tablespoon. Cream the egg yolks with $\frac{1}{4}$ oz butter ; strain the vinegar on to it. Thicken sauce in a bain-marie, gradually adding remaining butter. Set sauce aside.

To prepare the garnish : scald and skin tomatoes, cut in four, squeeze away the seeds and cut flesh into neat shreds. Slice the mushrooms and sauté in butter, with a squeeze of lemon juice and seasoning.

Strain the liquor from the fish, boil it to reduce it to 1 tablespoon and add it to hollandaise sauce with a teaspoon tomato purée, and the orange rind. Remove the skin and bones from the salmon, divide each steak in two and arrange in a warm serving dish. Add the garnish to the sauce and spoon it over the fish. The finished dish may be browned quickly under a hot grill, if wished, before serving.

Cheese soufflé

4 rounded tablespoons grated
  cheese
1½ oz butter
1 rounded tablespoon plain flour
salt
cayenne pepper
¾ cup of milk
1 teaspoon ready-made mustard
4 egg yolks
5 egg whites
1 tablespoon browned crumbs
  (raspings)

*7-inch diameter top (size No. 1)
  soufflé dish*

Ideally the cheese used should
be a mixture of grated Parmesan
and Gruyère. Otherwise use a
dry Cheddar.

Method
Rub inside of soufflé dish lightly
with butter and dust with browned
crumbs. Tie a strip of doubled
greaseproof paper round outside
of dish so that it comes 3 inches
above rim of dish and butter the
paper which extends above dish.
Set oven at 375°F or Mark 5.

Choose a medium to large
saucepan. Melt the butter, stir in
the flour off the heat, then cook
gently until straw-coloured.
Season well, blend in milk. Put
pan back on heat, stir until
boiling then draw aside. Add
mustard and beat in 3 rounded
tablespoons cheese and egg
yolks one at a time.
Watchpoint The basic sauce
must be well flavoured with
cheese and well seasoned to
compensate for the amount of
whites added.

When well mixed, whip egg
whites to a firm snow and stir 2
tablespoons of the whites into
the sauce, using a metal spoon.
Then stir in the remainder in
two parts, lifting the sauce well
over the whites from the bottom
of the pan. Turn the bowl round
while mixing ; do not overmix.

Turn lightly into prepared
soufflé dish. Quickly dust top
with crumbs and rest of cheese
mixed together. Bake for 25-30
minutes in pre-set oven, until
evenly-brown and firm to the
touch. Peel the paper away
from the outside and serve
immediately.

Cauliflower soufflé with mornay sauce

1 medium-size cauliflower
browned crumbs (for soufflé dish)
béchamel sauce (made with 1 oz
butter, $\frac{3}{4}$ oz plain flour, $\frac{1}{4}$ pint
flavoured milk)
3 egg yolks
4 egg whites
1 tablespoon grated Parmesan
cheese (for dusting)

For mornay sauce
1 oz butter
$\frac{3}{4}$ oz plain flour
$\frac{1}{2}$ pint flavoured milk (as for
béchamel)
2 oz grated cheese ($\frac{1}{2}$ Parmesan
and $\frac{1}{2}$ Gruyère)

*6-inch diameter top (size No. 2)
soufflé dish*

Method

Set oven at 375°F or Mark 5.
Butter the soufflé dish and dust
with browned crumbs. To allow
soufflé to rise above dish, tie
round outside a deep band of
greaseproof paper to come 3
inches higher than dish and
butter the part which extends
above dish.

Cut the cauliflower in four,
removing the hard stalk ; cook
in boiling salted water until
quite tender (about 10 minutes).
Drain well, refresh, and drain
again, then rub cauliflower
through a strainer (you should
have 6 oz cauliflower purée).

Prepare the béchamel sauce
and add the cauliflower purée
to it. (Alternatively place béchamel sauce in a liquidiser,
and add the cooked cauliflower
a little at a time.)

Beat the yolks into the cauliflower mixture one at a time.
Whip the whites to a firm snow
and fold into the mixture. Turn
into the prepared soufflé dish,
dust with the cheese, stand it
on the centre shelf of the pre-set
moderately hot oven and bake
for about 20-25 minutes until
well risen and brown. Meanwhile,
prepare the mornay sauce as
for a béchamel then draw it
aside and add the grated cheese.

The soufflé should be a little
soft in the centre. Peel the
paper off the outside and serve
immediately with the mornay
sauce handed separately.

Spinach soufflé

1½ lb spinach, or 1 large packet of
   frozen spinach purée
½ oz butter
salt and pepper
pinch of ground mace, or grated
   nutmeg
3 egg yolks
4 egg whites
1 tablespoon grated cheese
1 tablespoon browned crumbs

For sauce
1 oz butter
1 rounded tablespoon plain flour
salt and pepper
¼ pint milk

7-inch diameter top (size No. 1)
soufflé dish

This is a basic recipe for a
vegetable soufflé. Other vegetable purées — carrot, celeriac
— can be used instead of
spinach. Allow 8-10 rounded
tablespoons of purée to the
above quantity of sauce.

Method

Prepare the soufflé dish as for
cauliflower soufflé. Set oven
at 375°F or Mark 5.

Trim and wash spinach, boil
in salted water for 8 minutes,
drain and press well. Pass
through a sieve, turn back into
pan and stir over moderate heat
to drive off excess moisture.
Add the butter, season and set
pan of spinach aside.

If using frozen spinach, put
into a large pan on a gentle heat
until completely thawed. Then
increase heat to drive off excess
moisture, add butter, seasoning
and set aside.

To prepare sauce : melt the
butter, stir in flour off the heat,
then cook gently until straw
coloured ; season and blend
in milk. Add this to the spinach
with the mace or nutmeg and
additional seasoning to taste.

Beat in the egg yolks one at
a time. Whip the whites to a
firm snow, then cut and stir 1
tablespoon into the mixture
using a metal spoon. Stir in
remainder of whites and turn
into the prepared dish. Sprinkle
top with cheese and browned
crumbs mixed together. Bake
for 25-30 minutes in pre-set
oven until well risen and firm to
the touch.

Peel away paper from the
outside and serve immediately.

Stuffed aubergines (Aubergines farcies)

2 aubergines
4 lambs kidneys
1½ oz butter
2 medium-size onions (finely sliced)
1 dessertspoon plain flour
1 teaspoon tomato purée
¼ pint stock
1 clove of garlic (crushed with
    ½ teaspoon salt)
salt and pepper
1 bayleaf
½ lb tomatoes
2-3 tablespoons salad oil
1 tablespoon grated cheese (pre-
    ferably Parmesan)
1 tablespoon fresh white bread-
    crumbs

Method
Split aubergines in two length-ways, score round edge and across, sprinkle with salt and leave for 30 minutes to dégorger.

Skin the kidneys and cut out cores, cut in half lengthways. Heat a small sauté pan, drop in half the butter and, when foaming, put in the kidneys. Brown quickly on all sides then remove from the pan and keep warm. Lower the heat, add remaining butter and the onion. Cook for 2-3 minutes then draw aside. Stir in the flour, tomato purée and stock and bring to the boil. Add the crushed garlic to the pan with pepper, bayleaf and the kidneys. Cover and simmer gently for about 20 minutes.

Wipe the aubergines dry and sauté rather slowly in 2-3 table-spoons of oil until soft.

Watchpoint Aubergines brown very quickly when sautéd. If the flesh is browned before being cooked right through, complete cooking in oven.

Skin the tomatoes, remove the seeds and roughly chop flesh. When the aubergines are tender, scoop out the pulp with a spoon, leaving the skins intact.

Remove bayleaf from the kidneys, add the tomatoes and aubergine pulp and simmer together for 2-3 minutes. Set the aubergine skins in an oven-proof dish, fill with the mixture and dust the tops with the cheese and crumbs. Brown in a quick oven at 425°F or Mark 7 for approximately 7 minutes.

The stuffed aubergine halves after they have been browned in the oven

Aubergines Boston

2 even-size aubergines
olive oil
1 medium-size onion
1 oz butter
salt and pepper
5 oz cooked ham (thinly sliced
   and shredded)
béchamel sauce (made with 1 oz
   butter, 1 rounded tablespoon
   plain flour, $\frac{1}{2}$ pint flavoured milk)
1 tablespoon cream (optional)
1 oz cheese (grated)

If wished, the ham may be omitted.

Method

Split aubergines in two lengthways, run the point of a knife round the inside of the skin and score across the flesh. Sprinkle with salt and leave for 30 minutes. Dry the aubergines and fry in hot oil on the cut surface until brown. Put in oven at 375°F or Mark 5 for 5-10 minutes to soften completely.

Meanwhile chop the onion and soften in the butter in a covered pan. Scoop out the aubergine flesh carefully, chop it a little and add to the onion. Season, cook for a few minutes until soft, then add the ham. Put back into the skins and set on a baking tray. Prepare béchamel, adding cream, if wished, and coat aubergines. Sprinkle with cheese and brown in hot oven at 425°F or Mark 7 for 8-10 minutes.

Stuffed tomatoes valaisannes

6 large tomatoes
$7\frac{1}{2}$ fl oz milk
cayenne pepper
nutmeg
1 oz butter
1 oz plain flour
3 egg yolks
$\frac{1}{2}$ oz Gruyère cheese (grated)
2 egg whites
salt and pepper
chopped chives
white wine

Forcing bag and plain pipe.

Method

Scald, skin and cut off the tops of the tomatoes, scoop out the seeds and drain tomatoes thoroughly. Heat the milk, seasoning it well with cayenne and nutmeg.

To make soufflé-type filling, prepare a very thick béchamel sauce with the butter and flour and the seasoned milk. Beat in the egg yolks one at a time, followed by the grated cheese. Allow it to cool.

Whip the egg whites until stiff and fold into the sauce.

Season the tomatoes and sprinkle over a little chopped chives. Set the tomatoes close together in a gratin dish and sprinkle them with white wine. Pipe the soufflé mixture into the tomatoes and bake in a preset moderate oven at 350°F or Mark 4 for about 20 minutes.

Mushrooms in white wine

1 lb mushrooms
2 oz butter, or 3 tablespoons olive oil
2 large onions (finely sliced)
2 wineglasses white wine
bouquet garni
salt
pepper (ground from mill)
1 tablespoon chopped parsley

To serve
crisp rolls and unsalted butter

Method
Trim the mushrooms, wash quickly in salted water and cut in thick slices. Heat the butter (or oil) in a sauté pan, add the mushrooms, sauté over a quick heat for 1-2 minutes then remove from the pan. Reduce the heat, add the onions to pan and cook slowly until soft but not coloured ; tip on the white wine, add the bouquet garni and simmer until the wine is reduced by half. Return the mushrooms to the pan, season with salt and pepper from the mill and simmer for 5 minutes. Remove bouquet garni, tip the mushroom mixture into a hot gratin dish and dust with parsley.

Serve with hot crisp rolls and unsalted butter.

Italian broccoli au gratin

3-4 hearts of Italian broccoli (according to size)
grated cheese

For sauce
1 oz butter
1 shallot (finely chopped)
1 oz plain flour
$\frac{1}{2}$ pint chicken stock (free of fat)
1 dessertspoon French mustard (preferably Grey Poupon)
squeeze of lemon juice
1 egg yolk
2-3 tablespoons double cream

Italian broccoli or calabrese is well suited to a first course for a summer lunch.

Method
Wash broccoli thoroughly, then cook in boiling salted water for about 20 minutes until it is barely tender. Drain it well. Lay it in a well-buttered gratin dish and keep warm while preparing the sauce.

Melt butter in a pan, add chopped shallot and cook slowly to soften the shallot, then stir in the flour. Remove pan from heat, blend in the stock, return to heat and cook for 1-2 minutes, stirring continually. Mix in the mustard and lemon juice.

Blend together the egg yolk and cream, stir in a spoonful of the hot sauce, then add this liaison to the pan.

Before adding the liaison, make sure that the sauce is only just of coating consistency.

Draw pan aside, cool sauce for 1 minute, then beat in the cheese, reserving about 1 tablespoon. Coat broccoli with the sauce, sprinkle with remaining cheese and brown under the grill.

Eggs soubise

5-6 eggs
2 Spanish onions
little egg white
seasoned flour
deep fat (for frying)

For soubise sauce
$\frac{1}{2}$ lb onions (chopped)
1 $\frac{3}{4}$ oz butter
1 rounded tablespoon plain flour
$\frac{3}{4}$ pint milk

One of the best hot egg dishes. The creamy sauce contrasts well with the crisp brown onions.

Method
First make soubise sauce : blanch chopped onions, drain well and simmer in 1 oz butter until soft but not brown. Mix in an electric blender or rub through a strainer.

Melt remaining butter in a pan ; add flour off the heat, then add milk, and stir until boiling. Add the onion purée and cook for 4-5 minutes until creamy ; keep hot.

Slice Spanish onions and push out into rings, moisten with a little raw egg white and dust well with seasoned flour until they are dry. Fry in deep fat, taking care not to crowd the pan ; keep hot.

Poach the eggs and drain well. Arrange them in a dish, coat with the sauce and arrange the onion rings around them.

1 *Fry the onion rings in deep fat, being sure not to crowd the pan*
2 *Eggs soubise are covered with sauce and served with onion rings.*

Barbecued spare ribs

3 lb spare ribs
1 teaspoon salt
2 tablespoons soy sauce
1 tablespoon caster sugar
3 tablespoons tomato ketchup
2 tablespoons honey
1 cup of chicken stock (plus little extra for diluting marinade)

Method

Mix salt, soy sauce, sugar, ketchup, honey and stock well together and soak the spare ribs in this marinade for 1 hour.

Set oven at 375°F or Mark 5. Lift pork out of the marinade and put on a grid in a roasting tin holding a little water to prevent smoking. Roast in preset oven for about $1\frac{1}{4}$ hours, turning the spare ribs from time to time.

Put cooked spare ribs on serving dish. Dilute marinade with a little extra stock, boil up and pour over meat. Serve hot.

Spicy-flavoured barbecued spare ribs of pork served in a piquant sauce made from their marinade

Ravioli

Pasta makes a rather substantial starter, but in Italy that is its traditional place on the menu. Serve less than you would for a main course.

Ravioli consists of little rounds or squares of pasta filled with a savoury mince or a mixture of spinach and curd cheese.
To cook them, simmer in stock or water for 15-20 minutes, drain and cover with a good tomato sauce. Continue to simmer gently until golden. Serve with grated Parmesan cheese.

Ravioli paste

10 oz plain flour
$\frac{1}{2}$ teaspoon salt
1 $\frac{1}{2}$ tablespoons olive oil
2 eggs (beaten)
3-4 tablespoons milk, or water

Method
Sift the flour with salt on to a laminated plastic work top or board, make a well in the centre and put in the oil, eggs and half the milk or water.

Start mixing in the oil, eggs and water gradually, drawing in the flour, add the rest of the liquid as it is needed. Continue to work up the paste until it is smooth and firm, knead well, then cover with a cloth and leave for 20-30 minutes to get rid of any elasticity. Cut in half and roll out one piece, paper thin. Slide to one side, then roll out the second piece as thinly, brush with water and put out the chosen filling in teaspoons at regular intervals on the pastry. Lift the first piece on top and with a small ball of the paste press down the top piece around each mound of filling. Stamp out each one with a small fluted cutter or cut out in squares with a pastry wheel. Leave for 2-3 hours to dry a little. Then cook as described left.

Spinach and curd cheese filling

1 small packet of frozen spinach purée, or $\frac{1}{2}$-$\frac{3}{4}$ lb fresh spinach
2 oz curd, or cream, cheese
salt and pepper
small pinch of ground mace, or grated nutmeg

Method
If using frozen spinach, put into a pan and cook gently, stirring occasionally until firm. If fresh, boil, drain and dry ; sieve to a purée or chop very finely. Sieve cheese and mix in the spinach when cold. Season well and add spice. The mixture should be a firm purée.

Savoury meat filling

1 cup cooked chicken, or ham (minced)
2 tablespoons thick béchamel, or tomato sauce (sufficient to bind the meat)
3 teaspoons chopped mixed herbs, or parsley
1 egg yolk

Method
Mix ingredients together and season well. The mixture must be firm and quite stiff.

The ravioli paste is rolled out into two paper-thin rectangles

Spooning cooked spinach and curd cheese filling on to dampened paste

Cutting paste with a pastry wheel to form squares round the filling

101

Cannelloni

1 packet cannelloni (about $\frac{1}{2}$ lb)
— allow 3-4 tubes per person
$\frac{3}{4}$ pint thin tomato sauce
grated Parmesan cheese

For filling
$\frac{1}{2}$ lb raw veal, or pork (minced),
   or a mixture of both
$\frac{1}{4}$ pint béchamel sauce (made with
   1 oz butter, 1 oz plain flour,
   $\frac{1}{4}$ pint flavoured milk)
1 egg yolk
salt and pepper
pinch of ground mace, or grated
   nutmeg

Forcing bag and large, plain pipe

Method
First prepare filling. Make the béchamel sauce and leave to get quite cold before adding to the mince. Mix thoroughly, then add egg yolk and seasoning. The consistency must be quite stiff. Set filling aside.

Simmer the cannelloni in plenty of boiling salted water for about 7 minutes, then lift out carefully, dip into cold water, drain on cloth or absorbent paper.

Pipe filling into the cannelloni. Put them in a well-buttered flameproof casserole and pour over the tomato sauce (this should just cover). Bring to boiling point on top of stove, then cover and cook in the oven at 350°F or Mark 4 for 40-45 minutes. Ten minutes before end of cooking time, take off lid, sprinkle well with the cheese, increase the heat of oven to 375°F or Mark 5 and brown the surface. If preferred, the cannelloni may be served without browning, just sprinkled well with the cheese.

Tortelli

8 oz Ricotta, or curd, cheese
2 oz grated Parmesan cheese
1 egg
1 egg yolk
salt and pepper
pinch of allspice
1 tablespoon chopped parsley
ravioli paste
   (see page 100)
2-3 tablespoons melted butter
1-2 tablespoons grated
   Parmesan cheese

Method
Mix the cheeses together and beat until smooth, then add the egg and egg yolk, seasonings and parsley. Roll out the dough very thinly, stamp into rounds about $2\frac{1}{2}$ inches in diameter. Put 1 teaspoon of cheese mixture in the centre of each round, brush round the edge with water and fold over like a turnover, press edges down firmly and leave for 30 minutes.

Have ready a large pan of boiling salted water, put in the little turnovers and simmer for 15-20 minutes. Then lift out with a draining spoon, drain well on a cloth or piece of muslin, turn on to a dish, spoon the melted butter over them and dust well with the Parmesan cheese. Serve very hot.

Cold starters

Introduce your guests to their meal with a sweet and icy fruit salad, a rich, smooth pâté or a savoury mixture of meats, fish and salads set out on an hors d'oeuvre tray. Hot weather, habitually unpunctual guests, lack of time just before the meal for last minute preparation — there are all sorts of good excuses for serving some of the cold starters in this section. And if you can't think of a good excuse, just go ahead and serve one anyway, for you will find something to go with every meal.

Anchovy eggs

4 eggs
6-12 anchovy fillets
2 oz butter
black pepper (ground from mill)
$\frac{1}{2}$ pint thick mayonnaise
1 dessertspoon chopped mixed
   herbs — optional
watercress (to garnish)

Method
Hardboil the eggs, quickly cool them, peel and then cut in half lengthways. Remove the yolks and leave whites in cold water so that they will not become hard.

Soak the anchovies in milk to remove the excess salt, then drain them, unless they have soaked up all the milk, and pound until smooth. Work butter and egg yolks into anchovies. Season with black pepper.

Dry the egg whites and fill with the anchovy mixture ; sandwich the halves together again.

Serve the eggs coated with mayonnaise, lightly flavoured with the herbs. Garnish with sprays of watercress.

Eggs à la basque

8 eggs (hard-boiled)
4 large tomatoes (skinned)
6 caps of pimiento

For dressing
1 teaspoon paprika pepper
1 teaspoon tomato purée
$\frac{1}{2}$ clove of garlic (crushed with
   $\frac{1}{2}$ teaspoon salt and pepper from
   the mill)
2 tablespoons red wine vinegar
5 tablespoons salad oil
little sugar (optional)
2 tablespoons double cream

Method
Slice the hard-boiled eggs and cut the tomatoes in thin rounds. Shred the pimientos, keeping 2 shredded ones for garnish.

To make dressing : mix the paprika and tomato purée together, add the crushed garlic and mix to a paste. Add vinegar, then whisk in the oil and taste for seasoning. Add a little extra sugar if necessary (ie. if the vinegar is on the sharp side).

Place the eggs, tomatoes and pimiento in layers in a serving dish with two-thirds of the dressing. Finish with a layer of egg slices. Add the cream to the remaining dressing and spoon over top of the dish. Then cover the surface with a lattice of the reserved pimiento shreds.

Eggs à la grecque

6 eggs
6 oz smoked cod's roe
2 oz unsalted butter
squeeze of lemon juice
scant ½ oz gelatine
8 tablespoons tomato juice

For ½ pint mayonnaise
2 egg yolks
salt and pepper
dry mustard
¾ cup of salad oil
2 tablespoons wine vinegar

For tomato salad
1 lb tomatoes
½ teaspoon caster sugar

For French dressing
4 tablespoons salad oil
salt
black pepper (ground from mill)
juice and rind of ½ lemon

Method

Hardboil the eggs, shell them and keep in a bowl of cold water.

Prepare the **mayonnaise** by working the egg yolks and seasonings with a small whisk or wooden spoon in a bowl until thick; then start adding the oil drop by drop. When 2 tablespoons of oil have been added and the mixture is very thick, stir in 1 teaspoon only of the vinegar.

The remaining oil can now be added a little more quickly, 1 tablespoon at a time, and beaten thoroughly between each addition until it is absorbed (or if you are using an electric beater, in a thin steady stream). When all the oil has been absorbed, add as much of the remaining vinegar to taste, and extra salt and pepper as necessary.

Remove skin from cod's roe. Work butter in a bowl with a wooden spoon until soft. Cut eggs in half lengthways, remove yolks and push through a wire strainer. Keep whites in a bowl of cold water to stop them hardening. Pound the roe, butter and egg yolks together, adding lemon juice and 1-2 tablespoons of mayonnaise to make a creamy consistency. Fill egg whites, reshape each egg and arrange on a large plate. Scald and skin tomatoes, cut in thick slices and dust with sugar.

Soak the gelatine in the tomato juice, dissolve over gentle heat and add to the mayonnaise. Arrange the eggs on a serving dish. When the mayonnaise begins to thicken coat the eggs, using a large tablespoon, and let mayonnaise run from the bowl of the spoon. Mix together dressing of oil, seasonings and lemon juice and pour on to tomatoes ; place these around eggs on serving dish. Cut the lemon rind in fine shreds and cook in boiling water for 1 minute. Drain, dry on absorbent paper and scatter over the tomato salad.

1 *Pound cod's roe, butter and sieved yolks together in a mortar before adding lemon juice and mayonnaise*
2 *Fill egg white halves with mixture*
3 *Put filled halves together, then arrange them on a plate*
4 *After the dressing has been poured over the tomatoes, arrange them with the mayonnaise-coated eggs and scatter the strips of lemon rind over them*

Eggs dijonnaise

6 eggs (hard-boiled)
2 oz Cheshire cheese (finely grated)

For mayonnaise
2-3 egg yolks
salt and pepper
1 teaspoon French mustard
½ pint olive oil
2 tablespoons wine vinegar

For mushroom salad
¼ lb firm mushrooms
3 tablespoons olive oil
1 shallot (finely chopped)
1 tablespoon chopped parsley
1 tablespoon red wine vinegar
salt and pepper

Method

To make the mayonnaise : with a wooden spoon, work egg yolks with 2 pinches of salt, 1 of pepper and the mustard until thick. Then add 2 tablespoons of oil drop by drop to thicken mixture. Now carefully stir in 1 teaspoon of vinegar. Add remaining oil a little at a time, beating between each addition until it is absorbed. Then add remaining vinegar to taste and extra seasoning, if necessary.

Cut the eggs in half lengthways, remove the yolks and rub through a wire strainer into a bowl ; keep the whites in a bowl of cold water. Mix the yolks with the cheese and a tablespoon of mayonnaise and beat until smooth and creamy. Season to taste.

To prepare the salad : trim the stalks and wash mushrooms quickly in salted water, drain

Adding vinegar to the sauté mushrooms, shallot and parsley ; egg whites are kept in cold water to prevent them hardening

The mayonnaise is at the thick stage and the rest of the oil is slowly being added ; use some to mix egg yolks with cheese

well and cut in thick slices. Heat the oil in a sauté pan, add the mushrooms and shallot and cook briskly for 1 minute only, then pour into a bowl. Add the parsley, vinegar and seasoning and leave to cool.

Dry the halved egg whites on a cloth or absorbent paper, fill them with the cheese mixture and join the halves together; arrange on a serving dish. Spoon over the mustard mayonnaise and garnish with the mushroom salad.

Eggs dijonnaise arranged on a serving dish with mushroom salad

Artichoke and tomato salad

1 ½ lb jerusalem artichokes
salted water
squeeze of lemon juice
4-5 tomatoes (according to size)

For dressing
1 carton plain yoghourt
2-3 tablespoons double cream
salt and pepper
1 teaspoon caster sugar
squeeze of lemon juice
1 dessertspoon snipped chives, or
  chopped parsley

Method

Peel artichokes and cut into walnut-size pieces. Cook in pan of salted water with a good squeeze of lemon juice until just tender (about 7-8 minutes). Drain, rinse in cold water and drain again. Put in a bowl with tomatoes (skinned, seeds removed, flesh shredded).

To prepare dressing: turn yoghourt into a bowl, whip the cream lightly, add to yoghourt with the seasoning, sugar and lemon juice. Add chives or parsley. Mix together with artichokes and tomatoes.

Arrange in a salad bowl or hors d'oeuvre dish, and serve with brown bread and butter.

Avocado pear

½ avocado per person

For vinaigrette dressing
salt
black pepper (ground from mill)
1½ tablespoons white wine
  vinegar
5 tablespoons salad oil
squeeze of lemon juice
caster sugar (to taste)
1 teaspoon parsley (chopped)
½-1 green pepper (enough to
  give 2 tablespoons, chopped)
2 tablespoons spring onion
  (chopped)
6 black olives (stoned and
  shredded)

Method

Drop the chopped green pepper into boiling water, cook for 1 minute, then drain and rinse well with cold water.

To make dressing: mix a large pinch of salt and black pepper with the vinegar and whisk in the oil. Sharpen with lemon juice and add a little sugar to taste. Add other ingredients to the dressing.

Split the pears in half with a stainless steel or silver knife and remove the stone. Fill each half with the sharp vinaigrette dressing and chill slightly before serving on individual plates.

Avocado pear and tomato ice

3 avocado pears
1 can (14 oz) tomatoes
1 clove of garlic (crushed)
$\frac{1}{2}$ teaspoon salt
2 tablespoons caster sugar
pared rind and juice of $\frac{1}{2}$ lemon
3 sprigs of mint
1 stick of celery (sliced)
1 onion (sliced)
Tabasco, and Worcestershire,
    sauce (to taste)

Ice-cream churn freezer

This dish serves 6.

Avocado pear with tomato ice makes a Canadian-style party starter

Method

Tip the canned tomatoes into a pan, add the garlic, salt, sugar, lemon rind and juice, celery and onion and stir until boiling. Press tomatoes well, then add sprigs of mint. Cover pan and simmer for 5-10 minutes. Remove the mint and rub the contents of the pan through a nylon sieve. Allow to cool, add the Tabasco and Worcestershire sauces to taste. This mixture should be rather over-flavoured as freezing takes some of the flavour out.

Chill the mixture really well then turn into a freezer and churn until firm. Allow to ripen for 1 hour before serving.

For serving, slightly chill the avocados, cut in half and re-move the stone. Place a good scoop of the tomato ice in the cavity and serve immediately.

Pear and walnut salad

1 pear per person

For dressing
1 large egg
2 tablespoons caster sugar
3 tablespoons tarragon vinegar
1 small carton (2½ fl oz) double
  cream

To finish
1 lettuce
3 oz shelled walnuts (roughly
  chopped)

Choose ripe dessert pears such as Comice, William or Packham and allow 1 per person. The quantities are sufficient for 6 pears.

Coring a peeled, halved pear with a teaspoon

Method
To prepare the dressing: beat the egg and sugar until thoroughly mixed, then add the vinegar. Place the bowl over a saucepan of gently simmering water and stir until the mixture is thick. Remove from the heat and leave until cold. Whip the cream until it begins to thicken, then fold it into the dressing.

Cut the pears in half, peel them, and scoop out core with a teaspoon. Place each portion on a crisp lettuce leaf on a salad plate, and immediately spoon over the dressing. Scatter over the roughly chopped walnuts. Serve with brown bread and butter, or cheese sablés.

Cheese sablés

3 oz cheese (grated)
3 oz plain flour (sifted)
3 oz butter
salt and pepper
1 egg (lightly beaten)

Method
Cut butter into flour with a palette knife and, as soon as pieces are well coated with flour, rub in with your fingertips until mixture resembles fine breadcrumbs. Add cheese and season to taste. Press mixture together to make a dough. Flour, wrap dough in greaseproof paper, chill in refrigerator. Set oven at 375°F or Mark 5.

Roll out into a thin oblong. Cut into strips about 2 inches wide. Brush with beaten egg and cut strips into triangles.

Place sablés on a baking sheet lined with greaseproof paper, and cook in the pre-set oven for 10 minutes until golden-brown.

Tarragon cream dressing and chopped nuts make a pear salad delicious.
Serve with cold cheese sablés, as here, or brown bread and butter

Grapefruit and green grape salad

3 large grapefruit
6-8 oz green grapes
little caster sugar

For dressing
3-4 tablespoons olive, or salad, oil
about 2 tablespoons lemon juice
caster sugar and salt (to taste)
pepper (ground from mill)
1 teaspoon fresh, or bottled,
    mint (chopped)

Choose thin-skinned and heavy grapefruit.

Method
Cut the grapefruit in half and prepare in usual way. Dip grapes in boiling water, then peel and pip. To remove pips easily, flick them out with pointed end of potato peeler. Put 1 dessertspoon of grapes in the centre of each grapefruit half. Dust with sugar and chill.

To make dressing combine all the ingredients, whisk well. Taste and correct seasoning.

Pour a tablespoon of dressing over grapefruit before serving.

Pears in tarragon cream dressing

3-4 pears
lettuce leaves (optional)
paprika pepper (optional)

For tarragon cream dressing
1 egg
2 rounded tablespoons caster sugar
3 tablespoons tarragon vinegar
salt and pepper
$\frac{1}{4}$ pint double cream

Method
Prepare pears as for pear and walnut salad (page 112), omitting walnuts.

As an unusual alternative, try this recipe with avocado pears.

Grapefruit with mint ice

3 grapefruit
¾ pint water
pared rind and juice of 2 large
   lemons
4 oz lump sugar
2 large handfuls of mint leaves
   (picked from the stalk and well
   washed)
2-3 drops of green colouring
   (optional)
½ egg white (whisked)

To garnish
caster sugar
freshly chopped mint, or 1-2 leaves
   of crystallised mint

Crystallised mint leaves
Pick some fresh mint leaves,
wash and dry them carefully
and brush them very lightly
with lightly broken egg
white. Dust with caster
sugar and place on greaseproof paper or a cake rack
to dry for 1-2 hours. These
will not keep for more than
a day.

Method
First prepare the ice. Put the
water into a pan with the pared
rind of the lemons and the
sugar. Dissolve sugar over
gentle heat, then bring to the
boil and cook for 4-5 minutes.
Draw pan aside, add the mint
leaves and lemon juice.

Watchpoint Leave pan on
the side of the stove for liquid to
infuse ; do not boil as this would
spoil the flavour.

After 10-12 minutes, strain
liquid into a jug, taste for sweet-
ness and add colour, if wished.
Chill and then freeze ice, either
in a churn or in the ice-making
compartment of the refrigerator.
When the ice is just frozen to a
slush, add 1 teaspoon of
whisked egg white.

Prepare the grapefruit in the
usual way and hollow out the
centres a little to hold the ice.
Dust with caster sugar and chill.

To serve, put a scoop of the
ice on the centre of each grapefruit and sprinkle with a little
freshly chopped mint or 1-2
crystallised mint leaves.

Roquefort and walnut salad

2 lettuces (hearts only)
3 slices of white bread
1½ oz Roquefort, or other
    blue cheese (crushed)
6 large walnuts, or 12 half-kernels
8 tablespoons French dressing

Method

Wash and dry lettuces, chill until crisp. Cut crusts from bread and toast until golden-brown. When cold cut each slice into four and spread with the crushed Roquefort. Shell walnuts and, if wished, blanch kernels to remove skins. Make a French dressing.

Just before serving mix lettuce, walnuts and Roquefort 'toasts' with the dressing.

Tomatoes with Roquefort cream

8 even-size tomatoes
salt and pepper
2 eggs (hard-boiled)
3 sticks of tender celery (taken from
    centre of the head) — finely diced
3 oz Roquefort cheese
2 tablespoons double cream
4 tablespoons French dressing
1 teaspoon chopped chives

Method

Scald and skin tomatoes. Cut off the tops from the smooth end and carefully scoop out the seeds and core, using a tea-spoon ; drain and season the insides.

Chop the whites of the hard-boiled eggs and mix with the celery. Sieve the cheese and work half with the cream in a bowl. Combine celery mixture with this cheese and fill into the tomatoes ; replace the tops of the tomatoes 'on the slant'. Work the French dressing into the remaining cheese and add the chives.

Sieve the egg yolks on to a serving dish, set tomatoes on top and spoon over the dressing.

Charentais melon with grapes

8 small, or 4 large, charentais
  melons
1-1½ lb green, or muscat, grapes
lemon
little French dressing (made with
½ lemon juice in place of vinegar,
  and a little sugar)
freshly chopped mint

Method
Allow a whole or half charentais
per person, according to size.
If whole, cut a slice off the
flower end and scoop out the
seeds. If using as halves, cut
melons round like a grapefruit,
then flick out the seeds. Dip
grapes in boiling water then
peel and pip, put them in a
bowl and sprinkle with lemon
juice ; mix with French dressing.
Fill each half, or whole, melon
with the grapes and chill before
serving.

*Charentais melon is filled with
grapes tossed in French dressing*

Leeks vinaigrette

6-8 small leeks
1½ oz currants (soaked for 1 hour in
  boiling water)
2 tablespoons fresh tomato pulp, or
  1 tablespoon tomato purée diluted
  with 1 tablespoon water
2 tablespoons red wine vinegar
4-5 tablespoons oil
salt and pepper
caster sugar (to taste)

Method
Wash the leeks thoroughly and
cook them in boiling salted
water for 7-10 minutes, then
drain, refresh and drain again.
Drain and dry the soaked
currants. Put the tomato pulp
(or diluted purée) into a basin
with the vinegar, oil and
seasoning, mix together and
sweeten to taste with the sugar ;
add the currants.

Split the leeks lengthways
and arrange in a dish. Spoon
dressing over the leeks and
chill slightly. Serve with hot
fresh rolls and butter.

*Currants and tomato pulp added to
the dressing for leeks vinaigrette*

Artichokes vinaigrette

4 globe artichokes

For vinaigrette dressing
2 shallots (finely chopped)
6 tablespoons olive oil
2-3 oz mushrooms (finely chopped)
3 tablespoons white wine
2 tablespoons white wine vinegar
salt and pepper
squeeze of lemon juice (optional)
1 clove of garlic (optional)
3 oz ham (thinly sliced and finely chopped)
1 tablespoon chopped parsley, or chopped mixed herbs

Method
Trim off the points of the leaves of the artichokes with scissors and trim the stalk from the bottom. Plunge artichokes into boiling salted water and boil gently until a leaf can be pulled out (about 35-40 minutes). Then drain, refresh, and leave until cold.

Meanwhile prepare the dressing. Sauté the shallots slowly until just tender in 2 tablespoons of the oil, add the mushrooms and cook for 2-3 minutes. Turn into a bowl and leave until cool, then add wine, vinegar and remaining oil. Season well and add a squeeze of lemon juice if the dressing is not sharp enough. Flavour with a little garlic (crushed with salt), if liked, and add the ham. Leave

Chopped shallots, mushrooms and ham are mixed with wine, vinegar and oil to make a thick dressing for the artichokes

After some of the centre leaves and the chokes have been removed, the dressing is spooned into the cold artichokes

this to marinate for 15-20 minutes.

Prepare each artichoke by pulling out some of the centre leaves until the choke can be reached ; carefully scrape this away with a dessertspoon. Put a spoonful of the dressing in the centre of each artichoke, set them on individual dishes and dust with the chopped parsley or herbs.

The artichokes, filled with thick dressing, are served on individual plates

Mussel salad

2 quarts mussels
1 onion (sliced)
1 carrot (sliced)
1 wineglass white wine
$\frac{1}{4}$ pint water
bouquet garni
6-8 peppercorns
$\frac{1}{4}$ pint chicken stock
4 oz long grain rice
3 tablespoons oil
1 shallot (finely chopped)
$\frac{1}{2}$ bayleaf
1 head of celery
4 oz white mushrooms
juice of $\frac{1}{2}$ lemon
pepper (ground from mill)
4 tablespoons double cream
1 tablespoon chopped parsley

Method
Wash and scrub the mussels in several changes of water and place in a saucepan with the onion, carrot, wine, water, bouquet garni and peppercorns. Cover the pan and bring to the boil. Now shake the pan once or twice and simmer for 2-3 minutes, until all the mussel shells are open. Lift the mussels from the saucepan into a china bowl with a draining spoon and strain the liquid in the pan through muslin into another basin, measure and make up to $\frac{1}{2}$ pint with chicken stock.

Wash the rice and put in a pan with the oil and the shallot. Pour over the mussel liquor (mixed with stock) and bring to the boil, add the bayleaf, cover the pan and cook until the rice is tender and the stock absorbed (about 12 minutes).

Meanwhile wash the celery and cut into sticks about 1 inch long. Wash and trim the mushrooms, cut them in thick slices and leave to marinate in the lemon juice and pepper.

Some of the ingredients for mussel salad, and the salad being mixed

120

Take the mussels from their shells and remove the beards. Mix the mussels with the mushrooms and turn the rice into a bowl to cool. Drain and dry the celery. When the rice is quite cold, mix the celery, mussels and mushrooms into it with a fork, taste for seasoning and then add the cream. Pile into an entrée dish and dust with chopped parsley.

Crab salad printanier

1 medium-size crab, or 8 oz crab
  meat (frozen, or canned)
4 globe artichokes, or canned
  artichoke 'fonds'
2 tablespoons French dressing
rind and juice of 1 orange
2 oz black olives (stoned)
$\frac{1}{2}$ pint mayonnaise
4 large lettuce leaves

Method

Trim the artichokes and cook them in boiling, salted water for 35-40 minutes or until a leaf can be pulled out easily. Drain and refresh them. Pull out the centre leaves carefully, scrape away the choke and then remove each leaf, one by one, and discard. Spoon the French dressing over the hearts and leave them to marinate until cold.

Remove a strip of orange rind with a potato peeler, cut it in fine shreds and cook for 2-3 minutes in boiling water until tender ; then drain. Grate a little of the remaining orange rind.

Watchpoint The rind must be grated on the very finest side of the grater (nutmeg grater) ; make sure that only the zest is used and none of the pith.

Flavour the mayonnaise to taste with a little strained orange juice and the finely grated orange rind.

Arrange the lettuce leaves on individual salad plates, place an artichoke heart on top and cover with crab meat ; spoon over the mayonnaise. Garnish with shredded orange rind and olives, and serve with brown bread and butter.

Carefully removing outer leaves of the cooked artichoke ; centre leaves and choke have been pulled out

An unusual and savoury starter

Gratin of seafood

1¼ lb cod fillet, or 4 frozen cod
 steaks
juice of ½ lemon
2 oz button mushrooms
4 oz prawns (shelled)
½ pint milk
slice of onion
6 peppercorns
blade of mace
1 oz butter
1 oz plain flour
salt and pepper
1 tablespoon grated Parmesan
 cheese

4 individual gratin dishes

Method
Set the oven at 350°F or Mark 4.
If using fresh cod, discard the
skin and cut fillets into fine
strips. Grease 4 individual ovenproof gratin dishes (preferably
with butter), put in fish and
sprinkle with lemon juice. If
using frozen cod, thaw, place in
gratin dishes and sprinkle with
lemon juice.

 Wash mushrooms quickly in
salted water, trim away stalks
and then cut in fine slices.
Sprinkle mushrooms and prawns
on to the fish strips.

 Put milk in a pan with the
onion, peppercorns and mace,
warm and remove from heat.
Cover pan and leave to infuse
until milk is well flavoured (at
least 15 minutes). Strain.

 Melt butter in a saucepan,
remove pan from heat and blend
in flour, cook gently until straw-
coloured, then add flavoured
milk. Season, stir over gentle
heat until boiling, then simmer
for 1 minute. Adjust seasoning.

 Spoon sauce over the fish,
sprinkle with Parmesan cheese,
bake for 20-25 minutes in pre-set
oven until golden-brown.

Prawn cocktail

8 oz frozen prawns (allow at
 least 1½ oz per person)
1 small lettuce (finely shredded)
paprika pepper (for dusting)
4-8 prawns in their shells (for
 garnish)

For sauce
½ pint thick mayonnaise
1 dessertspoon tomato ketchup
salt and pepper
dash of Tabasco sauce
1 large tablespoon double cream
squeeze of lemon juice

Glass goblets for serving

Method
Thaw out prawns thoroughly.
Combine the sauce ingredients.
Add about half to the prawns,
just enough to coat nicely. Put
shredded lettuce in the bottom
of the goblets, arrange prawns
on top and coat with rest of
sauce. Dust with paprika and
garnish each serving with 1-2
fresh prawns, with the body and
tail shell removed but the head
left on.

Prawns Alabama

4-6 Dublin Bay prawns per person,
   or 10 oz frozen prawns
lemon juice
black pepper (ground from mill)
lettuce leaves
paprika pepper

For Alabama sauce
4 fl oz tomato sauce, or tomato
   ketchup, or tomato juice
$\frac{1}{2}$ pint very thick mayonnaise
1 small head of celery (chopped),
   or $\frac{1}{2}$ cucumber (finely diced)
1 small, or $\frac{1}{2}$ large, green pepper
   (seeds removed and flesh
   chopped)
1 rounded tablespoon freshly
   grated horseradish
1 clove of garlic (crushed with $\frac{1}{4}$
   teaspoon salt)
2-3 tablespoons double cream
few drops of Tabasco sauce

This Alabama sauce can also
be used as a dip for a cocktail
party.

Method

Shell the Dublin Bay prawns, or
thaw out frozen prawns. Sprinkle
over a little lemon juice and
black pepper, then cover and
leave to marinate while preparing the sauce.

Add tomato sauce (or ketchup,
or juice) to mayonnaise,
whisking it well. If using cucumber, sprinkle with salt and
leave for 15 minutes, then drain
thoroughly. Add it, or celery, to
sauce, with chopped pepper,
horseradish, garlic, double
cream and Tabasco. The sauce
must be quite spicy and piquant
— add more seasoning if necessary.

Arrange the drained prawns
on the lettuce leaves on individual plates and coat with 2-3
tablespoons of sauce. Dust with
paprika and serve chilled. If
you wish, shred the lettuce and
put in coupe glasses with the
prawns and sauce on top.

Tunny fish mousse

3 cans tunny fish (about 21 oz)
cold béchamel sauce (made with
 1½ oz butter, 1½ oz flour, 1 pint
 flavoured milk)
½ pint mayonnaise
1 oz gelatine
¼ pint vegetable stock, or water
salt and pepper
2 egg whites (stiffly whisked)

To garnish
1 small cucumber, or 1 head of
 celery
½ lb tomatoes
French dressing
1 teaspoon chopped mint

Ring mould (2 ½ pints capacity)

This quantity will serve 6-8
people.

Method
Lightly oil the mould.
  Drain the fish and pound
with the cold béchamel sauce
until smooth, then work in the
mayonnaise. Soak and dissolve
the gelatine in the stock (or
water) and add to the mixture,
season well. As the mixture
begins to thicken, fold in the
whisked egg whites. Turn
mousse into the mould and leave
to set.
  Peel the cucumber ; cut into
thick julienne strips, salt them
lightly, cover and leave for 30
minutes, then drain. Or wash
celery ; cut in julienne strips.
  Scald and skin the tomatoes,
cut in four and scoop away
the seeds. Mix the cucumber (or
celery) and tomatoes together,
moisten with French dressing
and add the mint. Turn the
mousse out of mould and fill
the centre with the salad.

Liver pâté

1½ lb pigs, or calves, liver
8 oz very fat bacon (unsmoked),
 or fat from cooked ham
2-3 tablespoons double cream
 (optional)
1 dessertspoon anchovy essence

For béchamel sauce
½ pint milk (infused with slice of
 onion, 6 peppercorns, 1 bayleaf,
 1 blade of mace)
1 oz butter
1 rounded tablespoon plain flour
salt
pepper (ground from mill)
pinch of ground mace, or nutmeg

*1 lb cake tin, or 6-inch diameter top
 soufflé dish (No. 2 size)*

Pigs liver is excellent for pâtés,
being rich and well flavoured.
Calves liver is more expensive
but more delicate in flavour.

Method
Remove any ducts and cut liver
into small pieces. Take two-
thirds of the bacon or ham fat,
cut into small pieces and pass
all through a mincer and / or
work in an electric blender.
  Make the béchamel sauce.
Season to taste, add ground
mace or nutmeg. Turn into a
dish and leave to cool.
  Mix the liver with béchamel
sauce, cream and anchovy
essence. Slice the rest of the
bacon or ham fat and use to line
the bottom of the shallow tin or
soufflé dish.
  If liver mixture is not very
smooth, pass it through a sieve
or mix in electric blender. Turn
into tin or dish, cover with foil,
set in a bain-marie half-full of
hot water. Bring to boil, then
put in oven, pre-set at 350°F or
Mark 4, for 45-50 minutes, until

firm to the touch. Cover with greaseproof paper, a plate or board and put a light weight (about 2 lb) on top and leave until the next day. Turn out and cut in slices for serving.

Watchpoint If pâté is to be kept for several days, cover top with a little clarified butter and keep in a cool place.

Cutting the liver into small pieces

Pressing the pâté with a 2 lb weight

Liver pâté is served with hot buttered toast and garnished with watercress

Chicken and calves liver pâté

8 oz thin streaky bacon rashers
(unsmoked)
4 oz chicken livers (sliced)
½ oz butter
1 clove of garlic (crushed with salt)
1 teaspoon chopped thyme
2 tablespoons chopped parsley

For farce
2 lb calves, or lambs, liver (in the
piece)
milk
8 oz pork fat (minced)
8 oz lean pork (minced)
2 shallots (finely chopped)
¼ pint double cream
2 eggs
salt
pepper (ground from mill)
1 small wineglass brandy, or
sherry
luting paste

Luting paste is a flour and water mixture of a consistency similar to that of scone dough. To seal a casserole or terrine, put 3-4 oz flour into a bowl and mix quickly with cold water to a firm dough (4 oz flour will take ⅛ pint water).

Method

Remove rind from the bacon, line a terrine with rashers. Sprinkle with a little of the brandy or sherry and grind over a little pepper from the mill. Set aside.

Remove any ducts and soak calves or lambs liver in milk for 2 hours. Then rinse and dry thoroughly. Cut in pieces and pass through a mincer. Mix with the minced fat, pork and the shallots. If possible work for a few seconds in an electric blender for additional smoothness. Mix in the cream, beaten eggs and rest of brandy or sherry. Season well.

Remove any ducts or veins from the chicken livers and slice. Sauté in butter for 2-3 minutes, add garlic and herbs and mix well.

Put half the farce into the terrine and scatter the liver mixture on the top. Cover with rest of the farce and put any remaining bacon rashers on the top. Cover with lid and seal round edge of lid with luting paste. Cook in a bain-marie in the oven for 1-2 hours at 325°F or Mark 3, until firm to the touch. Remove lid, press, using about a 2 lb weight, and leave to cool. Store in a refrigerator overnight. Turn out and serve in slices about ¼ inch thick. Serve with hot toast and butter.

Pâté bretonne

3 herrings (filleted and skinned)
1-2 tablespoons lemon juice
1 tablespoon finely chopped herbs
$\frac{1}{4}$ teaspoon ground nutmeg
$\frac{1}{4}$ teaspoon ground allspice
salt and pepper
clarified butter (for serving) — see
    page 140

For farce
4 oz rice
veal, or chicken, stock
3 hard-boiled eggs
2 herrings (filleted and skinned)
1 large mushroom (chopped)
1 egg (beaten)

Method

Set oven a 350°F or Mark 4.
    Marinate the 3 filleted herrings
in the lemon juice, herbs,
spices and seasoning while
preparing the farce.
    Bring stock to the boil and
cook rice in it for about 12 minutes, until tender ; drain and
leave to dry in a warm place.
    Pound the 2 herrings with the
yolks of the hard-boiled eggs,
mix in the cooked rice and
chopped mushroom and pass
this mixture through a fine sieve
or Mouli. Season and bind with
the beaten egg. Place half the
mixture in a buttered terrine and
arrange the marinated fillets
on top, then cover with the remaining farce. Stand the dish
in a bain-marie and cook in
pre-set oven for 45-50 minutes.
    Leave to get cold and pour
over a little clarified butter
before serving. Hand hot toast
and butter separately.

Country-style pâté 1

1 lb veal, or pork (minced)
8 oz pigs liver (minced)
4 oz pork fat (minced)
1 shallot (finely chopped)
1 large wineglass port wine
about $\frac{1}{4}$ of a small white loaf
    (crusts removed)
3 eggs (beaten)
small pinch of allspice
1 teaspoon marjoram, or thyme
    (chopped)
pinch of salt
6-8 rashers of streaky bacon

Medium-size loaf tin

Method

Set the oven at 350°F or Mark 4.
Put the veal and pigs liver, pork
fat and shallot into a bowl. Pour
the port over the bread and
leave until thoroughly soaked ;
add this to the meats with the
beaten eggs, allspice, herbs and
salt. Work together in electric
blender, or beat thoroughly.
    Line the loaf tin with bacon
rashers, fill with the mixture and
press well down. Smooth the
top, cover with foil or tie on a
double sheet of greaseproof
paper. Cook in a bain-marie for
$1\frac{1}{4}$-$1\frac{1}{2}$ hours in pre-set oven.
    The pâté is cooked when firm
to the touch. Cover with greaseproof paper and a plate or
board, then place a light weight
(about 2 lb) on top and leave
until cold. Then turn out and cut
into slices for serving, or store
covered with clarified butter.

Country-style pâté 2

1 lb veal (minced)
8 oz raw ham (minced)
1 lb pork (minced)
8 oz pigs liver (minced)
6 oz pork fat (minced)
2 cloves of garlic (crushed with salt)
good pinch of allspice (Jamaican pepper)
salt and pepper
1 wineglass brandy, or sherry
about 4 oz fat unsmoked bacon
1 bayleaf
clarified butter, or melted lard
luting paste (see page 128)

Method
Set oven at 350°F or Mark 4. Put minced meats and pork fat into a bowl, add the crushed cloves of garlic, allspice and seasoning. Moisten with the brandy or sherry.

Lay the fat bacon in the bottom of a terrine and put in the mixture. Press meat well down, smooth over the top and place the bayleaf on top. Put on the lid, seal edge with luting paste and cook in a bain-marie in the pre-set oven for about $1\frac{1}{2}$-$1\frac{3}{4}$ hours until pâté is firm to the touch.

Take out of oven, remove lid, place a sheet of greaseproof paper and a plate or board over it then put a light weight (about 2 lb) on top and leave until cold. Then cover with clarified butter or melted lard, and keep in a cool place until wanted.

Cod's roe pâté

12 oz smoked cod's roe (in the piece), or an 8 oz jar
1 teaspoon onion juice (from grated onion)
$\frac{1}{4}$ pint olive oil
1 cup fresh white breadcrumbs, or 3-4 slices of bread
1 Demi-Sel cheese
lemon, or tomato, juice (to taste)
pepper

To garnish
hot, dry toast
unsalted butter
black olives
lemon quarters

Method
Scrape the roe from the skin and put in a bowl with the onion juice. Pour the oil over the breadcrumbs and leave to soak for 5 minutes (if using slices of bread, remove the crust, put bread in a dish and sprinkle with the oil). Pound or beat the cod's roe with the Demi-Sel cheese until quite smooth, then work in the breadcrumbs and oil, a little at a time. Finish with lemon (or tomato) juice to taste and season with pepper. The mixture should be light and creamy.

Pile into a shallow dish and serve with hot dry toast (served between the folds of a napkin), unsalted butter, black olives and quarters of lemon in separate dishes.

1 *Scraping smoked cod's roe from skin into a mortar with onion juice*
2 *Pounding roe and Demi-Sel cheese, while breadcrumbs soak in oil*
3 *The pâté should be light and creamy*

Hors d'œuvre

Potato mayonnaise

$\frac{3}{4}$ lb potatoes (old or new)
French dressing (to coat
 potatoes)
about $\frac{1}{4}$ pint mayonnaise
pickled walnuts (sliced)
paprika pepper

Method
Boil potatoes in their skins,
then peel and toss them in
French dressing while still hot.
Small new potatoes can be kept
whole ; old potatoes should be
sliced. When cold, mix potatoes
with a little thick mayonnaise.
Season well ; put on serving dish.

Dilute 2 tablespoons mayonnaise with 1 dessertspoon hot
water to a coating consistency.
Spoon over the potatoes. Garnish round with sliced pickled
walnuts, sprinkle with paprika.

Cucumber salad

Peel 1 medium-size cucumber
and slice thinly ; salt lightly, then
press slices well between two
plates and leave in a cool place
for 1 hour before draining. Pour
over French dressing or spoon
over a little soured cream or
yoghourt. Sprinkle with snipped
chives.

Curried potato salad

about $\frac{3}{4}$ lb small new potatoes
 (cooked), or 1 small can
French dressing (to coat
 potatoes)
scant $\frac{1}{4}$ pint thick mayonnaise

For curry mixture
1 shallot, or $\frac{1}{2}$ small onion
 (sliced)
2 tablespoons olive oil
2 dessertspoons curry powder
1 teaspoon paprika pepper
$\frac{1}{2}$ cup of tomato juice, or
 2 teaspoons tomato purée
 mixed with $\frac{1}{2}$ cup of water
1 slice of lemon
1 dessertspoon apricot jam, or
 redcurrant jelly

Method
To make curry mixture : soften
shallot or onion in oil, then add
the curry and paprika ; cook for
1 minute, then add tomato
juice or purée, lemon, and jam
or jelly. Cover, simmer for 7-10
minutes, then strain. Keep this
mixture in a small jar or covered
container until wanted.

Have the potatoes ready,
cooked and tossed in French
dressing (see potato mayonnaise). If using canned potatoes, drain them thoroughly
and season with lemon juice,
salt and pepper. Add enough
curry mixture to flavour the
mayonnaise to taste. Put potatoes on a serving dish and coat
with the mayonnaise.

Rice, tomato and black olive salad

3 tablespoons long grain rice
$\frac{1}{4}$ lb tomatoes (ripe and firm)
2 oz button mushrooms
2 tablespoons water
squeeze of lemon juice
2 oz black olives (halved and stoned)
salt and pepper
2-3 tablespoons French dressing (made with dry white wine instead of vinegar)

Method
Cook rice in boiling, salted water for about 12 minutes, until tender ; drain, rinse, then dry in a warm place. Scald and skin tomatoes, quarter, and flick out seeds, then cut away the stalk. Cut each quarter in half lengthways.

Wash and trim mushrooms, quarter and cook for 2-3 minutes in the water with a good squeeze of lemon juice. Cook quickly, uncovered, so that liquid is well reduced by the time mushrooms are cooked ; shake and stir well.

Mix all ingredients with a fork, season well and moisten with French dressing.

Tomato salad with lemon dressing

$\frac{1}{2}$ lb tomatoes (ripe and firm)

For lemon dressing
1 tablespoon lemon juice
2 tablespoons oil
2 tablespoons single cream
$\frac{1}{2}$ teaspoon salt
1 rounded teaspoon caster sugar
pepper (ground from mill)
rind of $\frac{1}{2}$ lemon

Method
Scald, skin and slice tomatoes, then put them in a serving dish. Beat together dressing ingredients (except rind), and adjust seasoning. Cut lemon rind into fine shreds, blanch, drain and dry them ; sprinkle over the dish.

Spiced onions

$\frac{1}{2}$-$\frac{3}{4}$ lb button onions
$\frac{1}{2}$ lb ripe tomatoes
2 wineglasses white wine
3 tablespoons olive oil
salt and pepper
1 teaspoon fennel (finely chopped)
1 teaspoon coriander seeds

Method
Peel onions carefully, blanch for 7 minutes, drain and return to the pan. Skin tomatoes, squeeze out seeds, chop flesh roughly and add to pan with remaining ingredients. Cover pan and simmer gently for 40 minutes, when onions should be very tender but still whole.

Lift onions out carefully into serving dish. Strain the liquid over them and serve very cold.

Sweetcorn, pepper and pickled onion salad

1 large can sweetcorn kernels
salt and pepper
2 caps of canned pimiento
   (coarsely chopped)
1 tablespoon small pickled onions
   (quartered, or thinly sliced)
French, or lemon, dressing (as
   for tomato salad, page 133)

Some brands of canned sweet-corn already contain sweet pepper, in which case do not add pimiento.

Method
Drain sweetcorn well from its liquid ; put it into a bowl, season well and add the pimiento and the onions. Moisten sweetcorn mixture with the chosen dressing and turn into a serving dish.

Italian salad

2 oz pasta shells
$\frac{1}{4}$ lb ham (cooked and sliced)
2 oz black olives (halved and
   stoned)
2-3 tablespoons thick
   mayonnaise
1 teaspoon French mustard

Method
Simmer pasta shells in pan of boiling salted water for about 7 minutes or until just tender. Drain and refresh them.
   Shred the ham and mix this with the olives and pasta. Add mustard to mayonnaise and stir enough into the salad to bind it together.

Mushrooms Philippe

4-6 oz button mushrooms
1 large tablespoon olive oil
1 shallot (finely chopped)
1 wineglass red wine
1 teaspoon freshly chopped thyme
1-2 tablespoons French dressing
   (preferably made with red wine
   vinegar)
salt and pepper

Method
Wash and trim mushrooms (cut off stalks level with caps, slice stalks lengthways and put with mushroom caps).
   Heat oil in a small frying pan, put in the mushrooms and the shallot. Fry briskly for about 3 minutes, turning and stirring them all the time.
   Lift out mushroom mixture with a draining spoon into a bowl. Pour wine into the pan and boil until it is reduced by half. Add to the mushrooms with the herbs and French dressing. Season well, cover, and leave until cold.

Appendix

Notes and basic recipes

Asparagus (or sprue, the slender variety)

To prepare : trim the bottom stalks of the asparagus, leaving about 2-3 inches before the green starts. To make sure that all stalks are the same length, cut them while asparagus is still tied in bundles. After untying them, rinse stalks well in cold water and then, using a small vegetable knife, scrape the white part of the stems well and stand them in a bowl of cold water. Now tie the spears together in bundles, according to size, with fine string ; leave the cut stems standing in cold water until you are ready to cook them.

Have ready a deep pan of plenty of boiling salted water and stand the asparagus spears in this, stalk end down ; cook gently, covered, for 12-15 minutes or until the green part is tender.

Watchpoint The green tips should stand above the water and cook just in the steam.

Beans (haricot and butter)

Preparation and cooking :

1 Wash the beans and pick them over to remove any grit or small stones.

2 Soak them in plenty of tepid water for 8 hours, or leave overnight. If they have to be left longer, change the water or they may start to ferment.

3 Drain them, cover with plenty of fresh warm water and cook in a covered pan. If the water is hard, add a pinch of bicarbonate of soda which will help to soften the outer skins. Salt is never added at this stage as it would harden them. Bring them very slowly to boiling point, allowing 30-40 minutes, then simmer gently for about 1 hour. Drain them again and then use as specified in the recipe.

Breadcrumbs

To make crumbs : take a large loaf (the best type to use is a sandwich loaf) at least two days old. Cut off the crust and keep to one side. Break up bread into crumbs either by rubbing through a wire sieve or a Mouli sieve, or by working in an electric blender.

Dried crumbs : spread crumbs on to a sheet of paper laid on a baking tin and cover with another sheet of paper to keep off any dust. Leave to dry in a warm temperature — the plate rack, or warming drawer, or the top of the oven, or even the airing cupboard, is ideal. The crumbs may take a day or two to dry thoroughly, and they must be crisp before storing in a jar. To make them uniformly fine, sift them through a wire bowl strainer.

To make browned crumbs : bake the crusts in a slow oven until golden-brown, then crush or grind through a mincer. Sift and store as for white crumbs. These browned ones are known as raspings and are used for any dish that is coated with a sauce and browned in the oven.

French dressing

Mix 1 tablespoon wine, or tarragon, vinegar with $\frac{1}{2}$ teaspoon each of salt and freshly ground black pepper. Add 3 tablespoons of salad oil.

When dressing thickens, taste for correct seasoning ; if it is sharp yet oily, add more salt. Quantities should be in the ratio of 1 part vinegar to 3 parts oil.

For vinaigrette dressing, add freshly chopped herbs of choice.

Fried parsley

Choose 6-7 sprays of fresh parsley. Wash and dry well. Put the individual parsley sprigs into the basket.

Heat fat to normal frying temperature.

To avoid fat spluttering, turn off heat, then gently lower basket into the fat and fry for 1-2 minutes when parsley will be crisp and bright green. Drain on absorbent paper.

Grapefruit — preparation

To prepare grapefruit : halve, and using a small sharp knife, preferably with a curved and serrated blade, first cut out the core, then run the knife round the outside edge of the grapefruit, cutting between the flesh and the pith. Then slip knife either side of each membrane and lift out carefully without disturbing the segments of grapefruit. Carefully remove any pips.

Lobster

To kill a lobster : choose a sharp chopping knife. Lay the lobster out flat on a wooden board, hard shell uppermost. Have the head toward your right hand and cover the tail with a cloth. Hold lobster firmly behind the head with your left hand and with the point of the knife pierce right through the little cross mark which lies on the centre of the head. The lobster is killed at once.

To split a lobster : cut through the top part of the head, turn lobster round and continue to cut through the rear part of the head and down through the tail. Open out the two halves on the board and take out the dark thread (the intestine) which runs down the tail, and a small bag (usually containing weed) which lies in the top part of the head. These are the only parts to be thrown away. The greenish part, also in the head, is the liver which should be retained as it is considered a delicacy.

Mayonnaise

See recipe on page 106.

Mussels

Rinse mussels carefully in cold water. Examine them carefully and sharply tap any that are not tightly closed with the handle of a knife. If they do not respond by closing, discard them. Then scrub well with a small stiff brush and pull or scrape away any small pieces of weed from the sides. Rinse under a running tap, then soak them in a bowl of fresh water ; do not tip this water off the mussels as this might leave sand still in them, but lift them into another bowl or colander and wash again. When thoroughly clean, lift them out and put into a large pan for cooking.

If mussels have to be kept overnight, store in a bowl without water in a cool place and cover them with a heavy damp cloth.

Potato, creamed (for piping)

Boil peeled potatoes, drain and dry well. Mash or put through a Mouli sieve.

Gradually beat in boiling milk ($\frac{1}{2}$ pint to every $1\frac{1}{2}$ lb potatoes), with about 1 oz butter, and season to taste. This can be kept hot for up to 30 minutes by covering the levelled surface in the pan with 2-3 tablespoons of hot milk and the lid. Beat up before piping.

Redcurrant jelly

It is not possible to give a specific quantity of redcurrants as the recipe is governed by the amount of juice made, which is variable.

Method
Wash the fruit and, without removing from the stems, put in a 7 lb jam jar or stone crock. Cover and stand in deep pan of hot water.

Simmer on top of the stove or in the oven at 350°F or Mark 4, mashing the fruit a little from time to time, until all the juice is extracted (about 1 hour).

Then turn fruit into a jelly-bag, or double linen strainer, and allow to drain undisturbed overnight over a basin.

Watchpoint To keep the jelly clear and sparkling, do not try to speed up the draining process by forcing juice through ; this will only make the jelly cloudy.

Now measure juice. Allowing 1 lb lump or preserving sugar to each pint of juice, mix juice and sugar together, dissolving over slow heat. When dissolved, bring to the boil, boil hard for 3-5 minutes and skim with a wooden spoon. Test a little on a saucer : allow jelly to cool, tilt saucer and, if jelly is set, it will wrinkle. Put into jam jars, place small circles of greaseproof paper over jelly, label and cover with jam pot covers. Store in a dry larder until required.

Sauces
Béchamel sauce

Using the quantities given in the recipe, put the milk in a saucepan with a slice of onion, 6 peppercorns, a blade of mace and a bayleaf. Cover and heat gently, without boiling, for 5-7 minutes.

Pour off into a jug and rinse out the pan. Melt the butter in it and stir in the flour off the heat. Cook gently for a minute or so, until straw-coloured and marbled in appearance. Remove from heat and strain on a good third of the milk, blend and add remaining milk. When thoroughly mixed, season lightly, return to heat and stir until boiling. Boil for 2 minutes, then taste for seasoning. If wished, the sauce may be finished with 1 tablespoon of cream.

Tartare sauce
2 eggs (hard-boiled)
1 egg yolk (raw)
salt and pepper
$\frac{1}{2}$ pint oil
1 tablespoon vinegar
1 teaspoon chopped parsley
1 teaspoon snipped chives
1 teaspoon chopped capers, or gherkins

Method
Cut the hard-boiled eggs in half, remove the yolks and rub them through a strainer into a bowl. Add the raw yolk and seasoning ; work well together. Add the oil drop by drop, beating all the time, and dilute with vinegar as necessary. Finish off with the herbs and capers. If wished, add the shredded white of one of the hard-boiled eggs.

Tomato sauce
1 lb tomatoes, or 1 can (15 oz)
1 oz butter
1 rounded dessertspoon plain flour
$\frac{1}{2}$ pint stock, or water
bouquet garni
salt and pepper
pinch of granulated sugar
1 teaspoon tomato purée (optional)

Method
Melt the butter in a pan and stir in the flour off the heat. Cook gently for a minute, then remove from heat and blend in the stock or water ; stir until boiling.

Cut the tomatoes in half (after wiping them if fresh) and squeeze to remove seeds. Strain seeds to obtain juice only. Place tomatoes and juice in the saucepan and add bouquet garni. Season, add sugar, and tomato purée to strengthen flavour if necessary. Cover the pan and cook gently for 25-35 minutes until tomatoes are pulpy. Remove bouquet garni and turn sauce into a strainer. Press it through, return to rinsed-out pan, adjust seasoning and boil gently for about 5 minutes or until it is required consistency.

Watchpoint The appearance is improved by stirring in ½ oz butter just before serving. This will give the sauce a good gloss.

Scallops

Scallops, when alive, have their shells tightly closed, but they are usually bought ready prepared (opened and cleaned).

The easiest way to open them yourself is to put the shells into a hot oven for 4-5 minutes. The heat will cause the shells to gape. You must then carefully scrape away the fringe or beard which surrounds the scallop, attached to the flat shell, and the black thread (the intestine) which lies round it.

Slip a sharp knife under the scallop to detach it and the roe from shell. Scallops must be handled carefully as the roe is delicate.

Scrub each shell thoroughly ; these make good dishes to serve scallops in and can be used several times over.

Scallops take only 6-7 minutes to cook and, like all shellfish, should be simmered — not boiled (which makes them tough and tasteless). They can also be baked, fried or grilled.

Tomato pulp

To make ½ pint pulp, use ¾ lb ripe tomatoes in season or a 14 oz can of tomatoes. If using fresh tomatoes, cut them in half and remove seeds. Put tomatoes in a pan with a clove of lightly bruised garlic, a bayleaf, salt, freshly ground pepper and a slice of onion. Add a nut of butter, cover and cook slowly to a thick pulp (about 10-15 minutes). When really thick, pass through a strainer.

Adjust the seasoning and add a little sugar if necessary. The pulp should not be over sharp.

Tomatoes, skinning and seeding

To scald and skin tomatoes, place them in a bowl, pour boiling water over them, count 12 before pouring off the hot water and replace it with cold. The skin then comes off easily. To remove seeds cut a slice from the top (not stalk end) of each tomato, reserve slices, hold tomato in hollow of your palm and flick out seeds with handle of a teaspoon, using the bowl of the spoon to detach the core. So much the better if the spoon is worn and therefore slightly sharp.

Trout — preparation

The fishmonger will clean the trout for you, but the head should be left on. Wash it well and dry it on absorbent paper. With a pair of scissors, trim the fins close to the skin. The tails can be trimmed neatly or 'vandyked' (cut into a 'V' shape). If the fish is large, score once or twice on each side.

Glossary

Bain-marie (au) To cook at temperature just below boiling point in a saucepan standing in a larger pan of simmering water. May be carried out in oven or on top of stove.

Blanch To whiten meats and remove strong tastes from vegetables by bringing to boil from cold water and draining before further cooking. Green vegetables should be put into boiling water and cooked for up to 1 minute.

Bouquet garni Traditionally a bunch of parsley, thyme, bayleaf, for flavouring stews and sauces. Other herbs can be added. Remove before serving dish.

Butter, clarified Butter cleared by heating gently until foaming, skimming well, pouring off clear yellow oil, leaving sediment (milk solids) in pan.

Dégorger To remove impurities and strong flavours before cooking. It is done by sprinkling the sliced vegetable with salt, covering with heavy plate, leaving up to 1 hour, and draining off excess liquid.

Infuse To steep in liquid (not always boiling) in warm place to draw flavour into the liquid.

Julienne strip Strip of vegetable/meat cut about $\frac{1}{8}$ inch by $1\frac{1}{2}$-2 inches long.

Liaison Mixture for thickening/binding sauce/gravy/soup, eg. roux, egg yolks and cream, kneaded butter.

Marinate To soak raw meat/game/fish in cooked or raw spiced liquid (marinade) of wine, oil, herbs and vegetables for hours/days before cooking.

Mirepoix Basic preparation for flavouring braises and sauces. Diced vegetables, sweated (cooked gently for a few minutes in butter), to draw out flavour. Diced ham or bacon and bayleaf sometimes included.

Roux (white, blond or brown) Fat and flour liaison. This is the basis of all flour sauces (white/brown). The weight of fat should be slightly more than that of flour.

Slake To mix arrowroot/cornflour with a little cold water before adding to a liquid for thickening.

Sauté To brown food in butter or oil and butter. Sometimes cooking is completed in a 'small' sauce - ie. one made on the food in the sauté pan.

Sweat To draw out flavour by cooking diced or sliced vegetables gently in a little melted butter in covered pan until softened (5-10 minutes).

Seasoned flour Flour to which salt and pepper have been added.

Sprue Slender variety of asparagus.

Velouté Of a velvety consistency, achieved by pouring a well flavoured fish, veal or chicken stock on to a blond roux.

Index

141